equal parts cocktails

equal parts cocktails

the simple ratio for spectacular drinks

fred siggins

photographs by kristoffer paulsen

"In a world where cocktail bars and the drinks made in them have become more like wild science experiments, this book brings us back down to earth and back to basics. With *Equal Parts Cocktails,* Fred Siggins allows us to remember that great drinks can indeed be simple and perhaps if we spend less time making the drinks, we can spend more time enjoying them. This book casts a wide net, focusing on classics that we know and reimagining other classics in equal parts, as well as throwing in some new cocktails we may have never heard of. Buy this book. Enjoy your drinking. You'll be happy you did!"

—Ivy Mix, author of *Spirits of Latin America* and *A Quick Drink,* cofounder of Speed Rack, and co-owner of Whoopsie Daisy and Fiasco!

"Fred Siggins is a scholar—of spirits and chemistry and the fine art of bartending, but also of the *culture* of drinking. It's remarkable, then, that he has deployed his deep expertise to make a book that shows how simple it all can actually be, demystifying the formula at the root of some of the world's most magnificent cocktails. This is exciting for all, but particularly great for me: a person who hates memorizing recipes and loves to drink exceptionally well."

—Lesley Suter, brand director at Eater

TEN SPEED PRESS
California | New York

It is perhaps no surprise that my true appreciation for equal parts cocktails only crystallized once I began working alongside Sasha Petraske at Milk & Honey in NYC. Given that Fred and I share a lineage that stretches from the pioneering bars of New York to the vibrant cocktail scene in Melbourne, our perspective on global trends like the equal parts movement was always going to be similar.

As I worked through classic recipes, a connecting thread soon became clear: The ones that held my attention, and those that consistently achieved perfect balance, were almost always built on an equal parts ratio. The trend only continued through the 2013 launch and my years of operating Attaboy.

For bartenders in training, these drinks acted as an absolute foundation. They provided instant confidence; while a newer bartender might have to dig deep to remember the specs for other drinks on the ticket, the simplicity of the equal parts recipe was a surefire success—a spec they could execute perfectly, every time.

There is a true beauty in their simplicity and memorability. They are so easy to remember that any level of bartender, novice or pro, can whip one up with style. Better yet, the modifications are endless! The DNA of the equal parts family is clear in its lineage: The Last Word (page 78) served as my direct inspiration for the Paper Plane (page 114), which itself provided the framework for the modern classic, the Naked and Famous (page 124). That is quite the creative family tree!

foreword

The fact that these drinks now firmly command their own category in the modern lexicon, standing proudly alongside Manhattans, sours, and Old Fashioneds, makes me tremendously happy.

With this guide, Fred Siggins has made this homage to a very necessary cocktail category incredibly easy to navigate. This is not a guide meant to slow you down with excessive science or overly complicated theories. Instead, the recipes are presented in an approachable way, and simple variations are explained so you can easily modify your drink, your way. It is, essentially, a cocktail choose-your-own-adventure.

Above all, it's *fun.* We love fun anecdotes while we sip on old cocktails, and Fred's historical notes tap brilliantly into all this curious history. This book is an essential piece of the modern cocktail library.

Sam Ross

Bartender and Cofounder of
Attaboy New York & Nashville

**Welcome to *Equal Parts Cocktails*—the easiest drinks recipe book you'll ever read! Within these pages, you'll find cocktail recipes with simple formulas in which all the ingredients have the same measurements. They're easy to make and easy to remember, and you don't need any prior knowledge of cocktails or bartending. None of the drinks in this book require homemade ingredients or hours of prep work; all you need are just a few simple tools and techniques, plus items you can find at your local liquor store or supermarket.

If the idea of making good cocktails at home sounds daunting, don't worry, it's a lot easier than it seems. Strip away all the fancy tools and techniques professional bartenders use, and all you're doing is putting a couple of different liquids in a glass. With the recipes in this book, you won't even need to remember measurements and ratios, because they're all exactly equal!

I have a terrible memory for recipes. So, like many in my profession, especially when I was starting out, I found the concept of equal parts cocktails to be a blessing. No more remembering how many dashes of this or barspoons of that, no need to know if this drink has a 1:2:3 ratio of ingredients or a 1:3:5. With equal parts drinks, it's simply a 1:1:1 ratio, and away you go.

Even after many years as a professional bartender, I still know only a few classic cocktails by heart. But when it comes to equal parts recipes, I've got a whole treasure trove. So with this experience in mind, have no doubt that I will soon have you making excellent cocktails with ease.

Despite their simplicity, these recipes also allow for plenty of experimentation and modification to fit your specific tastes. In each recipe, you'll learn which ingredients offer sweetness, sourness, bitterness, and other key flavors. So, if you like things a bit sweeter or a bit more sour, you can easily adjust to your liking with a little more of this, a little less of that. And if you're missing an ingredient, I'll show you the best way to swap it for something with a similar flavor profile. I'll cover how to present your drinks perfectly with easy garnishes, how to choose appropriate glassware, and even how to make cocktails in bulk ahead of time so you can serve a group of friends and still relax when it's party time.

Each section will cover a different style of cocktail, starting out with the all-time classics that everyone has heard of, such as the Negroni (page 53), the Margarita (page 65), and the Martini (page 50), as well as many of their variations. From there, we'll look at some lesser-known classics that all bartenders rely on, like the Corpse Reviver #2 (page 74) and the Last Word (page 78). Next, we'll delve into some party favorites from the 1980s and '90s, including the Cosmopolitan (page 95), the Japanese Slipper (page 99), and the Espresso Martini (page 96), which are still popular for very good reason, and—if made right—can be truly delicious.

Once we've nailed the drinks everyone knows, we'll get into modern classics like the Paper Plane (page 114) and the Jungle Bird (page 119), and we'll explore the creativity of some of the world's best bars and bartenders mixing up delicious drinks around the globe today. Throughout every section, there will be fun stories and anecdotes, because the true art of bartending isn't wasting brain space with complicated recipes; it's keeping yourself and your guests entertained with a simple, well-made drink and a good story to tell.

getting started

Before we get to the recipes, let's set you up for success. Here you'll learn all the basics of preparing great cocktails at home, starting with the tools, techniques, and skills you'll need. I also include plenty of pro tips to help your drinks really shine, teach you what glassware to use, and show you how to stock your home bar so you can make the cocktails you love whenever you desire.

tools of the trade

All the equipment bartenders use regularly to make cocktails is listed below. This can range from the inexpensive utensils found at your local pub to the super-fancy specialized bar tools that professionals rely on. You don't have to spend a lot of money to get the basics, and there are plenty of common household items you can use in a pinch—especially when it comes to measuring. Bar tools can be as utilitarian or aesthetic as you like, so find what works for you.

jigger

An indispensable tool in the bar world, a jigger is a small metal cup that comes in many different shapes and sizes for measuring liquor and other liquid ingredients. With equal parts cocktails, you don't even have to know exactly how much liquid you've got, as long as it's the same for every ingredient. You can use anything you have on hand—a shot glass, for example, or a small measuring cup. But a one-ounce jigger is a cheap and easy thing to find, and most drinks in this book will call for one ounce of each ingredient, so it will be a handy thing to have.

shaker

A shaker is what we often use to mix cocktails. There are many different kinds, but I find the easiest ones to use are shaker tins: a set of one larger and one smaller tin that fit together. Some people use a heavy pint glass in combination with a large tin for shaking, but I don't like using them because the glass is heavy and breakable. If you're fancy, you can use a Parisian shaker or a three-piece shaker, both of which look beautiful on the bar.

JIGGERS

TWO-PIECE SHAKER TINS

MIXING GLASSES

BARSPOONS

In a pinch, you can use anything with a good enough seal for shaking cocktails. For example, I find sports drink bottles and protein shaker bottles work well because they have a wide opening for adding ingredients and ice, they stay sealed, and they're light enough to shake hard.

mixing glass

This is what we use for stirring classic cocktails like the Martini (page 50) and the Manhattan (page 56) that don't need to be shaken. Most bars just use a basic, heavy-bottomed pint glass, but you can also get beautiful specialized ones that are generally a little bigger so you can make more than one drink at a time. They also tend to be a little heavier, making them harder to knock over.

If you don't have a specialized mixing glass, you can use any large, heavy glass with a wide opening and straight sides, or even a glass or ceramic pitcher. Many bartenders just use the larger tin of a two-piece cocktail shaker. If you do that, be sure to hold the bottom while you're mixing so it doesn't tip over, because they're a lot lighter and less stable than glass.

barspoon

This is a long, thin spoon to help you stir cocktails in a mixing glass. It's also useful for fishing garnishes out of jars. If you don't have a barspoon handy, a chopstick or the handle of a wooden spoon works just fine. But, as barspoons are inexpensive and also good for measuring small amounts of liquid, I recommend getting one.

hawthorne strainer

After we've shaken or mixed a drink, we use this strainer to pour it into the glass we'll drink from. It holds back all the chunks of ice while allowing the liquid to pass through. Practice holding the shaker tin and Hawthorne strainer in one hand, with your thumb and three fingers holding the shaker close to the top, and your index finger keeping the strainer in place. This keeps your other hand free to use a fine strainer (see below) should you need it.

fine strainer

This is a mesh strainer we use when we want to remove any little chunks of ice or bits of fruit from a drink to make it nice and smooth. It's generally used by pouring the drink through a Hawthorne strainer held in your strong hand, through the fine strainer in your other hand, and into the glass.

juicer

The recipes in this book call for a lot of freshly squeezed citrus juice, so you'll need something on hand to extract the juice from whole lemons, limes, oranges, and grapefruit. I prefer the simple glass or stainless steel kind with a ridged cone in the middle because you can keep them steady on a countertop and push down hard to get the most juice, but use whatever kind you feel comfortable with.

peeler

A peeler is a great thing to have on hand for making garnishes of fresh citrus peel, which feature heavily in this book because they smell so good and add bright colors for beautiful cocktails.

bar knife

A sharp knife is also an invaluable tool for cutting up fruit and other garnishes. You'll generally want something small and very sharp, like a paring knife, but in a pinch, a serrated steak knife works well. Make sure you have a stable surface to cut on, like a cutting board.

blender

To make frozen drinks like the Piña Colada (page 91) and Frozen Strawberry Daiquiri (page 107), you'll want to have a good blender on hand. You don't necessarily need a top-of-the-line blender like a Vitamix, but you will need one that is powerful enough to crush ice and puree fruit. A small, personal blender works well for single-serve blended cocktails, too.

ice molds

Cocktails require a lot of ice, so if you have the kind of freezer that prepares ice automatically, you're probably good to go. If not, be sure you have extra ice molds on hand to stock up before a party. I like large, square, silicone ice molds because they're easy to use and make big chunks of ice. Large ice cubes melt very slowly, so they are great for both shaking and serving cocktails.

STRAINERS

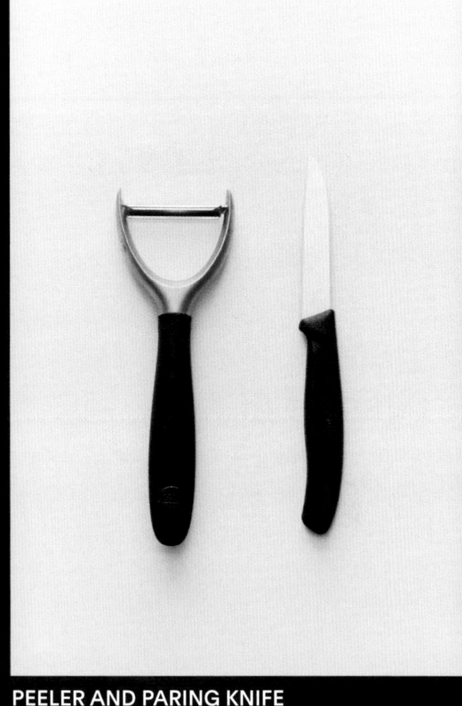

PEELER AND PARING KNIFE

ICE MOLDS

JUICERS

how to make a cocktail

When putting together a cocktail, there are three things you're trying to do: **mix** the ingredients, so everything is nicely integrated and every sip tastes the same; **chill** the drink so it's nice and cold; and **dilute** the alcohol a little bit to make it more palatable. Those are the basic factors of making any cocktail. For the recipes in this book (as for most cocktails), we're going to achieve these goals of mixing, chilling, and diluting our cocktails in one of four ways: **build**, **stir**, **shake**, or **blend.**

build

This is the most basic way of preparing a cocktail. To build a cocktail, all we're going to do is add the ingredients one at a time to the same glass we'll be drinking from. Chances are, you've done this plenty of times. A basic example is a gin and tonic, where you'd simply add the gin to the glass you want to use, fill it with ice, top it up with tonic water, and give it a bit of a stir.

We generally use this option when making long drinks (sometimes called tall drinks), which are drinks served in a tall glass and topped up with some kind of soda. We also build spritzes, like the Aperol Spritz (page 54), which are made in a wineglass and topped up with sparkling wine, and it's also an easy and quick way to make simple cocktails like the Negroni (page 53).

stir

Stirring is an important technique for drinks like the Martini (page 50) and the Manhattan (page 56) that don't include any mixers or juices. We're talking about the classic, boozy cocktails that appear mostly in the first chapter of this book. We use this technique to mix, chill, and dilute cocktails that are going to be served "straight up" (without ice) in a cocktail glass, but also for some drinks that are served "on the rocks" (with ice) in a tumbler.

To stir a cocktail, you'll need a mixing glass, a barspoon, and a Hawthorne strainer (see page 13). For this technique, we're going to add all the ingredients to our mixing glass and fill it at least halfway up with ice (you want the ice to be much higher in the mixing glass than the liquid).

Using the barspoon, stir until the drink is nice and cold and all the ingredients are mixed together. This kind of stirring isn't the same as if you were stirring a soup in a pot. It's more like stirring sugar into a coffee—all you're really doing is using the spoon to move the ice around the glass in a circle. To do this, start by sliding the back side of the spoon all the way down one side of the glass so it's sticking straight up and resting in between the inside surface of the mixing glass and the ice. Then, place your fingers at the top of the spoon and turn it gently around the inside of the glass a few times. You'll see that it takes the ice with it as it turns, giving you a nice smooth rotation of all the ingredients.

Do this until the outside of your mixing glass starts to feel cold—that's how you know your drink will be cold, too. You can also use the spoon to taste the drink to see if it's diluted enough. Use the spoon to put a little bit of the drink on the back of your hand and taste it from there to make sure the spoon stays clean (and to look like a pro!).

How much dilution you want in your cocktail is a matter of personal preference, but basically, if the drink tastes too harsh to you, stir it some more, and if it tastes watery, you've overdone it a little. Err on the side of less dilution, because you can always stir more, but you can't undo dilution! How quickly a drink dilutes is based on a lot of factors, like how big your ice is, how warm the room is, and so on. I like to use large chunks of ice and keep my mixing glass in the freezer to help slow the rate of dilution and give me a bit more control.

Once you're happy with how your drink is chilled and diluted, use a strainer to pour the liquid, but not the ice, into your desired glass for serving the cocktail.

shake

This is the one method that everyone has seen at their favorite bar. It's fun, it's loud, and it lets everyone know you're making a cocktail! The reason we shake instead of stir some cocktails is because, in addition to mixing, chilling, and diluting them, we also want to aerate them a little—give them some texture, make sure everything is really well incorporated, and maybe even get a nice bit of froth on top when you shake really hard.

We generally use this technique for drinks that include some kind of fresh juice. Fruit juices naturally don't mix with alcohol very well, so we need to put some effort in to get them to combine properly.

To make a shaken cocktail, you'll need a set of shaker tins, a Hawthorne strainer, and sometimes a fine strainer as well. Add all your ingredients to the

STIRRING A COCKTAIL

SHAKING A COCKTAIL

OPENING THE SHAKER TINS

smaller side of the shaker tin set, fill it up with as much ice as possible, then close the shaker using the other, larger side (or the cap if you're using a three-piece shaker tin). Make sure the sides of the two shaker tins line up along one vertical plane so there's a straight line from top to bottom on one side.

Next, pick up the shaker with both hands and shake it hard for about ten seconds. The biggest mistake people make with shaking is that they move themselves a lot, but not the cocktail! Try to plant your feet shoulder-width apart and keep your all movements below the elbows while the rest of your body remains relatively still.

The idea is to get the ice in the shaker to travel hard and fast along the whole length and smash into the top and bottom over and over. You should hear the classic *clack clack, clack clack* sound as the ice hits the ends of the tins with each shake. You'll know the cocktail is ready when the tin gets frosty.

To open, place the shaker vertically with the large side down. Hold it in your dominant hand right where the two parts meet and smack it with the butt of your other hand directly opposite where you're holding. You should feel the top part of the shaker sort of pop, and then you can remove it easily, leaving all the liquid in the bottom part. If that doesn't work, hold the shaker against your body for support, and use your other hand to wiggle the top off.

Once your shaker is open, use your Hawthorne strainer to strain the liquid into your glass. In this book, if a recipe simply says "strain," just use the Hawthorne strainer. But if it says "fine strain" you'll want to use the Hawthorne strainer and the fine strainer, pouring the liquid through both to catch any little bits of ice or fruit pulp. See the photos for how to hold the strainers properly.

blend

There are certain drinks that demand to be blended, like the Super-Simple Frozen Margarita (page 66), Piña Colada (page 91), and Frozen Strawberry Daiquiri (page 107), so having a good blender on hand is pretty useful, especially if you're mixing for a group.

You can turn almost any cocktail into a refreshing, slushy frozen drink with a high-quality blender. My bartending colleagues and I used to play a game called "blend a classic" in which we'd put any classic cocktail we could think of into a blender with ice.

The most important thing to remember about blending is that to get a good texture, you need about twice the volume of ice as total liquid in the drink. For example, if you have a drink with four ounces of ingredients in total, which equals half a cup, you'll want one cup of ice.

Blended drinks often require a little more sweetness to taste balanced, so if you're trying to blend a recipe from this book that doesn't specifically say to blend it, you might want to add a splash of a simple syrup.

pro tips

To make your drinks really hit pro level, follow these easy tips that professional bartenders use to make every cocktail taste great.

use lots of ice!

Ice is probably the most important ingredient in any drink recipe, and cocktail bars go through a *lot* of frozen H2O. At high-end bars, you'll even hear mixologists talking about their "ice program"—their strategy for making, processing, and using all different kinds of ice to make perfect drinks every time. Cocktails are better when they're colder, so when making drinks, never skimp on the rocks. A normal ice cube tray from your freezer might be enough for one or two drinks, but if you're going to be making more, plan ahead by using multiple ice cube trays. In a pinch, you could always purchase bagged ice.

When you're using a mixing glass or a cocktail shaker to make a cocktail, you want to fill it all the way up with ice cubes, even if you're making just one drink. If you're serving a tall drink over ice, like a gin and tonic, add the liquor first, then fill the glass to the top with ice before adding your mixer. The more ice you have, the colder your drink will be and the slower the ice will melt. If you just have one or two ice cubes floating around in all that liquid, it will melt quickly, and your drink will be tepid and watery.

If you're making something like an old-fashioned cocktail or just having a whiskey on the rocks, one big chunk of ice is the best option as it will melt a lot slower and stop your drink from becoming watery. At home, I use large silicone ice molds (see page 15) to make big cubes of ice that are great for serving on-the-rocks drinks. I keep a couple of them in the freezer, and once they're frozen, I pop them out into a larger container. Then, I refill the molds so I always have plenty on hand.

You can also make large chunks of ice by filling something like a plastic take-out container with water and freezing it. You can then break it up into useable chunks by taking the ice out of the container, wrapping it in a towel, and giving it a couple of whacks with a hammer or mallet on a hard, stable surface.

fresh citrus is best

In this book, when I mention lemon or lime juice, I always mean freshly squeezed. This is one of the big differences between a proper craft cocktail and something you might get at a dive bar or out of a premix. At professional cocktail bars, we spend hours juicing fresh citrus because nothing else tastes as good. Note that fresh citrus juice only lasts about twenty-four hours. After that, it starts to oxidize and the taste changes dramatically from bright and fresh to soapy and flat. When you're making drinks, it's best to juice your fruits as close to mixing time as possible, and throw out any leftover juice after a day, or freeze it to use for cooking.

Sweet-and-sour mix and bottled citrus juices are fine in a pinch, but for the purposes of this book we're going to keep it classy. So, if any of the recipes in this book call for citrus juice, make sure you have plenty of whole lemons or limes on hand for squeezing—the juicier the better.

think about balance, and don't be afraid to play around

All the recipes in this book call for equal parts of every ingredient, but that doesn't mean you can't experiment and balance drinks to your own preference. Each recipe will have some combination of these components:

- **a base spirit:** This is the base of your cocktail, also known as the "strong" element. It'll be something like vodka, tequila, or whiskey.

- **a sweet element:** All cocktails have a bit of sweetness, such as a liqueur or maybe a syrup of some kind, to counterbalance the booze and add extra flavor.

- **a sour element:** This is almost always lemon or lime juice, which offsets the sweet element and makes the cocktail nice and refreshing.

- **a bitter element:** This will be something like an amaro that can add welcome bitterness and complexity to a drink.

- **a "weak" element:** Some drinks will call for something like orange juice, pineapple juice, or soda water. These things don't really affect the balance of the drink; they're just there for extra flavor or to give the cocktail some additional volume. You don't really need to worry about these elements throwing off the proportions of a drink.

With this knowledge, you can play around with the flavor profiles. If you like drinks a little more sour, bump up the citrus juice or drop down the sweet element a little. If you like things a little sweeter, reduce the citrus or bitter elements a little or beef up the sweeter ingredients like syrups and liqueurs. The beauty of equal parts drinks is that they're flexible, so play around with a little more of this, a little less of that, and make them how you're going to enjoy them best.

I'll give you an example: The Amaretto Sour (page 67) calls for equal parts whiskey, amaretto, lemon juice, and egg white. In this drink, the amaretto is the sweet part and the lemon juice is the sour part. If you like your drinks sweeter, add a little more amaretto. If you like your drinks less sweet and more sour, increase the lemon juice. Easy squeezy.

Understanding how each element influences the others gives you more flexibility, meaning you don't need to have the exact ingredients on hand to make great cocktails, as long as you're replacing like for like. For example, if you don't have any gin, you can make the same drink with vodka, white rum, or tequila (all "strong" elements), and it will still work. No whiskey on hand (or you just don't like whiskey)? Try it with dark rum or brandy instead. As long as the proportions are the same, the drink should still balance out nicely.

The same goes for the sweet element. The Margarita (page 65), for example, calls for an orange liqueur like Cointreau as the sweet element. But it works just as well if you replace that with an apricot liqueur, a berry liqueur, or even Midori (melon liqueur). Obviously, the taste will change, but since all these liqueurs have a similar amount of sugar, the drink will still be balanced. Don't try it with Kahlúa, as the combination of coffee liqueur and lime juice might be a bit weird, but anything sweet and fruity will work really well in this example, including fruit-flavored syrups.

This is basically how bartenders come up with new drinks—playing around by replacing one element with another while maintaining the overall proportions. So, once you've nailed a couple of the recipes in this book, start exploring! And don't feel like you have to buy a whole new cabinet of random spirits. Use what you have on hand and what you most enjoy drinking.

glassware

Glassware is an important part of the cocktail experience. After all, what's a martini without a martini glass? That being said, you need only four different kinds of glassware on hand to make every drink in this book look and taste great. But at the end of the day, if you prefer drinking martinis from rocks glasses—or even from a plastic bucket!—that's up to you. For example, Manhattans are mostly served straight-up in a stemmed cocktail glass, but you could just as easily use a small tumbler. I like them on the rocks in a tumbler because it dilutes them slightly and makes them last a little longer. So don't stress if you don't have the perfect glass—use whatever you have on hand.

With any style of cocktail, it's a good idea to chill your glassware ahead of time, as it will keep your drink colder for longer. To do this, just pop your glass in the fridge or freezer for at least a half hour before use. This is especially important for straight-up drinks like martinis, Manhattans, and daiquiris because they don't have any ice in the glass to help keep them cold.

cocktail glass

For the purposes of this book, whenever I say "cocktail glass," I mean any small-volume, stemmed glass designed for straight-up cocktails (meaning served with no ice or mixer). This could be a traditional V-shaped martini glass, a curved Champagne coupe, or a classic cocktail glass like the Nick & Nora design that's popular in many cocktail bars. As long as it has a stem— which will keep your hand from warming the drink—and can hold four to five ounces of liquid, it will work as a cocktail glass. To get the best results, it's especially important to chill this style of glass before making your cocktail, because it won't hold any ice to help keep the drink cold.

highball glass

A highball glass is essentially a tall tumbler, like you might use to drink juice or iced tea. We use these glasses for simple mixed drinks like vodka sodas, as well as cocktails that are topped up with a mixer, like the Mojito (page 59).

Basically, you just need a glass that's big enough to fit your cocktail along with plenty of ice and some soda, but not so big that you drown it with mixer. About twelve ounces is perfect for most recipes. For drinks with a lot of ingredients, like the Long Island Iced Tea (page 104), you'll need a sixteen-ounce pint glass.

rocks glass

A rocks glass is a short, squat tumbler that's big enough to fit a cocktail plus plenty of ice. This is the kind of drink we use for cocktails served "on the rocks"—that is, over ice. Classics like the Old Fashioned and the Negroni (page 53) are usually served in rocks glasses, as are modern shaken drinks like the Jungle Bird (page 119). For this glass, you're looking for something around eight ounces, but it doesn't have to be exact!

wineglass

Wineglasses are great for spritz-style drinks like the Aperol Spritz (page 54) but also work well when you're serving pitchers of cocktails to a group of friends. Just make sure you're using wineglasses that have enough room for some ice and soda, ten to twelve ounces or more.

specialty glassware

Of course there's an endless array of specialty and antique options out there, from ceramic tiki mugs shaped like *Star Wars* characters to vessels created for specific cocktails, like copper mint julep cups. Don't stress about having the exact right glass for every drink, but of course if you enjoy collecting—have fun! If you're a fan of frozen cocktails in particular, it might be worth getting a set of margarita coupettes or hurricane glasses for your slushy summer drinks.

STEMMED COCKTAIL GLASSES

HIGHBALLS OR "TALL" GLASSES

TUMBLERS OR "ROCKS" GLASSES

SPECIALTY GLASSWARE

how to stock
a home bar

Walk into your average cocktail bar, and you'll see bottles of all shapes and sizes lining the shelves—hundreds of them, representing every conceivable combination and brand a customer might desire. But you don't need all that to prepare great drinks at home. By investing in just a few key bottles, you can build a great home bar collection and make most of the recipes in this book. The most important thing to remember is to stock your bar for the drinks you want to make. Don't like gin? Avoid it! Love tequila and mezcal? Get five different ones! It's your bar and your money, after all. Below is a simple guide—organized by base spirits, cocktail flavor makers, miscellaneous ingredients, and garnishes—so you can stock your bar and make the drinks you like.

the basic spirits

At most bars, the "basic" spirits that are always in stock are vodka, gin, rum, tequila, bourbon, and Scotch whisky. These are the ones that people tend to ask for the most often in simple mixed drinks, like a bourbon and Coke or a gin and tonic, and they are the foundation of the most popular cocktails.

vodka

This is the "cleanest" of spirits—that is, it's light, clear, and almost tasteless. Usually made from a highly processed grain base like wheat or corn, it's basically pure ethanol (the kind of alcohol we drink) diluted with water. This type of super-clean and clear spirit was first popular in Poland and Russia during the late Middle Ages and became more and more refined over the years. It eventually made its way to the West after the Communist revolution in Russia in the early twentieth century.

The story goes that Vladimir Smirnov (who was friends with the Russian royals) fled during the revolution with nothing but the shirt on his back and the recipe for his vodka. It eventually ended up in the hands of an American company and was renamed Smirnoff. The rest is history.

Vodka is a hugely important part of the modern cocktail story and is a base for many of the drinks in this book. The great thing about vodka is that it enhances the flavors you mix it with without imparting much of a taste of its own, giving you a lot of flexibility to create light but full-flavored drinks.

I recommend a good bottle of Polish rye-based vodka like Belvedere for a great texture and less hangover than cheaper brands. Of course, Tito's is also a favorite if you want to support an American-made brand.

gin

Gin is a weird one to have ended up on the speed rail of every bar in the world, as it's basically a British version of a juniper-flavored medicinal tonic from Holland. Gin as we know it today is a clean and clear spirit infused with botanicals, or plant-based flavorings. The main plant ingredient is juniper, the berry of an alpine evergreen bush native to the mountains of Europe. The taste and smell of juniper is piney, resinous, and savory, so gin is often preferred by people who like bitter, complex, and aromatic flavors more than sweetness.

Gin has made a massive comeback in recent years after being considered pretty uncool during the 1990s and early 2000s. Now you can't walk three feet without stumbling into a new craft gin brand. Given the abundance of different brands, if this is a spirit you love, it's worth having a few different styles on your home bar. You might opt for something bold and juniper-forward like Beefeater, as well as something light and floral like Hendrick's.

The only way to figure out what you like is to go out and try them, but if you want to keep it simple, a good bottle of London Dry–style gin (which sticks with classic botanicals such as juniper and citrus) such as Beefeater or Tanqueray will cover almost every occasion, from martinis to fun and fruity concoctions, and will also work great in a simple gin and tonic.

There are also more modern styles we call "contemporary gin," (see the Semper Fizz on page 147). It's a bit of a loose term, but generally these gins don't conform to the traditional London Dry–style and instead embrace New World flavors, regional ingredients, and unique botanicals. Explore the gin shelf at your local liquor store and find something fun and interesting, especially a brand that features more floral elements or South Asian spices like cardamom and ginger.

rum

Rum is made from sugarcane, and apart from that, there aren't a lot of rules. In general, it can be "white" or "silver" with no color, "gold" or "pale" with a small amount of aging in oak barrels (or with just some flavoring or coloring added for effect), or "dark" or "black" with a significant amount of woody flavor from aging in oak barrels.

Rum can generally be broken down into four categories: Puerto Rican or Cuban (Spanish-style), Jamaican (English-style), agricole (French-style), and cachaça (Brazilian-style). If you want to know what style a rum is, just think about the language they speak in the place it's made.

Spanish-style rum is the most common, as it's the cheapest to make. It's the lightest in flavor and the most commercially successful, with the most famous brand being Bacardi. This style of rum is great for light and bright Caribbean classics like the Mojito (page 59) and the Frozen Strawberry Daiquiri (page 107).

Jamaican-style rum, also made in other English-speaking places in the Caribbean like Barbados, tends to be bigger, bolder, and funkier in flavor, aroma, and texture. These rums are great for tropical punches and fruity cocktails in which you want that nice richness to come through.

Agricole rums are the least common and are primarily popular in France and the French-speaking Caribbean islands—mostly Martinque—where they're made, but a well-stocked liquor store should have at least one or two brands. These rums are big and funky like their Jamaican cousins, but are less sweet and have a more savory, grassy note to them. They're wonderful for when you want a full-flavored daiquiri, or when you're combining multiple styles of rum for complex punches, like the Mai Tai (page 60).

Cachaça is the national spirit of Brazil, consumed in popular cocktails like the caipirinha. Similar to agricole rums, cachaça is made from fresh cane juice rather than molasses, but it tends to be more highly refined and less expensive while still maintaining a nice, grassy flavor.

There's also spiced rum, but that's a whole different thing, flavored with spices like vanilla and usually with a bunch of sugar added, so we're not going to worry about that one.

If you love rum and tropical cocktails, it's worth having a selection of the above varieties. But for a basic home bar setup, one bottle of good white Spanish-style rum like Havana Club or Flor de Caña plus a bottle of Jamaican dark rum like Myers's or Appleton Estate 8 Year Old Reserve would be enough to get you started.

tequila and mezcal

Made in Mexico from the blue agave plant, tequila is one of the fastest-growing spirits categories in the world right now, and everyone loves a good margarita, so unless you really hate the stuff, having at least one high-quality bottle on your home bar should be a priority. The problem with tequila is that there are a *lot* of substandard products out there, and some of it is expensive (hello, celebrity endorsements). The best advice I can give is not to worry about slick marketing or beautiful packaging; instead, ask someone from your local craft bottle shop or cocktail bar to point you in the right direction.

Tequila can be "white" or "silver"—sometimes called "blanco," "joven," or "plata"—meaning unaged and clear in color. This kind is best for when you want your cocktails to be light and bright. "Reposado" (rested) tequilas have spent a short time aging in oak barrels, so they'll have an amber color and a slightly woody taste. They often offer a touch more mellowness and complexity at the expense of brighter, fresher flavors. "Añejo" (aged) and "extra añejo" tequilas have spent a lot more time in oak barrels, so the woody flavors will start to dominate, almost like a whisky or brandy. These are best for sipping on or using in richer cocktails like a tequila Old Fashioned.

Mezcal, which can be made from any kind of agave plant, is a whole other category of Mexican spirit that's becoming more and more popular. Mezcal tends to be less refined and more intense in character than tequila, and with a broader range of flavors that can include smoky, mineral, grassy, fruity, and earthy. If you like tequila, it's a great idea to explore this incredible spirit, especially if you're into bigger, bolder flavors.

To make sure you can prepare a great margarita any time, have a bottle of good-quality silver tequila like Arette or Siete Leguas on your home bar. And if you're a real tequila lover, stock a bottle of reposado as well. To dip your toe in the mezcal waters, add a bottle of artisanal mezcal like Derrumbes to your shopping list—just avoid the cheap stuff! With mezcal, you really get what you pay for.

bourbon and rye whiskey

Bourbon, America's native whiskey, is a must-have on any bar. Made primarily from corn and aged in new, heavily charred American oak barrels, bourbon is sweet, punchy, and woody, making it perfect for cocktails of all kinds. There are so many brands on the market that it can be hard to know where to start, but a good rule is that if you wouldn't drink it straight, you shouldn't use it in your cocktails. I usually opt for a traditional, no bells and whistles whiskey like Old Forester or Wild Turkey.

It's also a good idea to have a bottle of rye whiskey, another spirit with American roots, on your bar for things like the Manhattan (page 56). Rye is made from rye grains (as the name implies), so it's dryer and spicier than

bourbon but supplies the same woody punch. For something super easy to work with, you can't go wrong with Michter's Straight Rye, but if money is a consideration, Old Overholt works every time.

scotch and irish whisk(e)y

The word *Scotch* refers to whisky (spelled with no "e") made in Scotland, usually from malted barley. It's generally more textural and less woody than bourbon, but the range of styles is huge, from light and floral to rich and smoky. Scotch comes broadly in two forms: blended and single malt.

Blended Scotch is usually what we're talking about when it comes to cocktails because it's inexpensive, consistent, and easy to work with. Think brands like Dewar's, Johnnie Walker, and Chivas Regal. We'll use blended Scotch in cocktails like the Cameron's Kick (page 86) and the Rusty Nail (page 49).

Single malt, on the other hand, tends to be more expensive and bolder in flavor and texture, so people generally prefer to sip this style neat. But if you don't mind big flavors and money isn't a worry, there's nothing wrong with making cocktails from single malt! If you want to introduce some smokiness to your whisky cocktails, try Talisker 10 Year, and if you prefer richer, sweeter single malts, go with something like Aberlour or Glendronach.

Irish whiskey is another common style and, of course, hails from Ireland. Most Irish whiskies are easy-drinking blended styles like Jameson and Bushmills, which are great for cocktails and mixed drinks, but there are also more traditional single pot still Irish whiskies, which are a bit richer in texture, and single malts, with bigger, bolder flavors like their Scottish counterparts.

There are heaps of other whisky styles to experiment with, from Japanese to Canadian to myriad small-scale producers popping up all over the world. But a decent bottle of blended Scotch whisky like Johnnie Walker Black Label or Dewar's 12 is a great place to start when making cocktails.

brandy

Even though you won't find brandy on the speed rail of most bars (it's pretty rare for someone to order a brandy and Sprite these days, but you should try it—it's delicious), this is still an important spirit in the cocktail world. It's a key ingredient in numerous classics, like the Brandy Alexander and the Sidecar (page 63).

Brandy is essentially a fruit-based spirit. The most famous kind is Cognac, a type of brandy from France made with grapes and aged in oak barrels, often for decades. But you can also get grape brandy that's unaged (like grappa from Italy and pisco from Peru) or brandy made with other fruits, like apples or peaches.

There are so many kinds of brandy, and the flavors are so diverse, that it would take many chapters to describe them all. For the purposes of this book, we'll stick with Cognac as it's by far the most common. A decent bottle like Hennessy VS or Pierre Ferrand will be perfect for most cocktails. We'll also use applejack—an American apple brandy—for drinks like the Manhattan (page 56); Laird's is a good brand that's easy to find.

the cocktail flavor makers

Now that we've got our basic spirits sorted out, we need to spice things up a little. These are the most common ingredients that professional bartenders employ to introduce complexity and depth to cocktails, as well as to impart the big, fun flavors that people love. A lot of these components are used to add sweetness (like liqueurs and syrups), while others supply bitterness (such as amaro and bitters), and others are just there for a bit of sophistication (like sherry and absinthe). All of these ingredients are critical to making your cocktails taste more flavorful and interesting.

liqueurs

Liqueurs are sweet spirits that have had a fair amount of sugar added, along with other flavors from ingredients such as fruit, nuts, coffee, or herbs and spices. There is a huge number of different liqueurs on the market, and they're a great way to add interesting flavors, complexity, and sweetness to cocktails. As such, you'll see various types of liqueurs throughout this book.

The most common liqueurs are fruit-flavored, like Cointreau (orange), Midori (melon), and apricot brandy. There are also nut liqueurs such as amaretto (a sweet almond-flavored spirit), coffee liqueur (such as Kahlúa), and all sorts of other dessert-flavored liqueurs like mint, chocolate, and hazelnut. The French are known for making great liqueurs and will often call them "crème," as in "crème de cassis," which is a blackcurrant liqueur. Peach schnapps, cherry brandy, and Curaçao are all examples of fruit liqueurs, so the names can be a bit confusing, but as long as it's sweet and has a bold flavor added, it's a liqueur!

A number of liqueurs are more complex, with multiple flavors, herbs, and spices added to them. Some great examples that will be used in this book include Chartreuse, a French herbal liqueur with bright, vegetal notes, used in the Last Word (page 78), and Drambuie, a honey and whisky liqueur that tastes like Christmas and shows up in the Rusty Nail (page 49).

amaros

Amaros are a very special group of flavored liqueurs that are sweet but also bitter. They feature heavily in this book because they can add a lot of complexity to simple cocktails. Even if you don't really like bitter things, amaros are still an important tool—a dash here or there goes a long way! The most famous example is Campari, a bittersweet orange-flavored liqueur that's used in countless cocktails, like the Negroni (page 53) and the Jungle Bird (page 119).

Most amaros come from Italy, where there are hundreds of different styles and brands. Along with light and bright amaros like Campari and its less-potent sibling Aperol, there are also intensely bitter and herbal ones like Fernet-Branca (used in Foo Fighters, page 142), earthy, vegetal ones like Cynar (used in the Manhattan, page 56), light and fruity ones like Montenegro (used in Buckley's Chance, page 141) and Nonino (used in the Paper Plane, page 114), and floral ones like Suze (used in the White Negroni, page 131).

If you try these amaros on their own, you might love them, but you might also find them a bit overpowering. But when mixed in a cocktail in the right way, they can work magic. Amaros are an especially important part of modern cocktail making as more options become available outside of Italy and craft producers in other countries come up with unique styles. Every time you see an amaro in a recipe in this book, try switching it out for another one and see what happens!

vermouth

Vermouth is a kind of fortified and aromatized wine. That means the original wine has had some spirit added to it to make it more shelf-stable and has had aromatic herbs and spices added to it for extra flavor and for their natural preservative effect. Vermouths are a critical ingredient in many, many classic cocktails like the Martini (page 50), Negroni (page 53), and Manhattan (page 56), so if that's the kind of drink you like, a couple of bottles of good vermouth will be key to your home bar.

There are two primary kinds of vermouth: sweet and dry. Sweet vermouth is made from red wine, has a bit more sugar, and tends to include rich, warm spices like vanilla. Dry vermouth is made from white wine and, as the name implies, tends to be much less sweet and include brighter, more floral botanical flavorings. For sweet vermouth, I'd opt for a bottle of Punt e Mes, Dolin Rouge, or Carpano Antica Formula—all excellent quality for mixing or sipping neat. For dry vermouth, Noilly Prat or Dolin Dry are my go-tos.

Off-dry vermouth is another important ingredient in cocktails in this book and is used in a number of recipes, including the White Negroni (page 131) and the Tsukikage Martini (page 151). It's white-wine based, but sweeter and fruitier than dry vermouth. You can read more about off-dry vermouth on page 75. For an off-dry vermouth, brands like Lillet Blanc or Cocchi Americano Bianco will work perfectly and are also delicious on the rocks with a wedge of grapefruit on a sunny afternoon.

Rosé vermouth is, you guessed it, made from rosé wine. It's also somewhere in between sweet and dry vermouth in terms of sweetness and richness, so, much like the off-dry styles, it's a good one to have on hand if you like spritzy, springtime cocktails like the Aperol Spritz on page 54.

An important thing to remember about vermouth is that even though it's fortified with preservatives, it's still a wine, so it will go bad eventually. Once you open a bottle of vermouth, keep it in the refrigerator properly sealed to stop it from oxidizing. If it's been open for more than three months, dump it and get a new one. Vermouth tends to be relatively inexpensive, so there's no point saving old stuff. And if you ever walk into a bar and see opened bottles of vermouth on the shelf and not in the fridge, don't expect a good martini!

sherry

Sherry is a really misunderstood kind of wine, but it's something modern bartenders rely on a lot to add complexity to cocktails. Sherries are a group of Spanish fortified wines that are stronger in alcohol and more intense in flavor than regular wine. They range in flavor from very dry and floral to very sweet and sticky.

For the cocktails in this book that include sherry, like the London Calling (page 127) and the Tsukikage Martini (page 151), we're going to use the medium-bodied dry variety called "fino" (refined). Even if you don't like the taste of sherry on its own (try it with a bit of hard cheese, and it'll rock your world), it's a wonderful addition to many drinks. Like vermouth, sherry will last longer than a normal wine, but not forever, so properly seal the bottle once it's opened and keep it in the refrigerator.

syrups

Syrups are a common ingredient in cocktails to add sweetness and flavor without any additional alcohol. We won't be using too many syrups in this book, because a lot of the ones used by professional bartenders are homemade, and we want to keep things simple by using commercially available products.

However, a few basics like simple syrup will be important to have on hand for certain recipes. You can make it yourself or you can buy premade versions. To make simple syrup, combine equal parts white sugar with boiling water in a heatproof container and stir until the sugar has fully dissolved. Allow to cool completely before transferring to a clean glass bottle and storing in the refrigerator pretty much indefinitely.

Other basic syrups often found in bars are things like orgeat, an almond-flavored syrup featured in the Mai Tai (page 60); grenadine, a pomegranate syrup used in cocktails like the Tequila Sunrise; falernum, a spiced lime syrup found in many tropical-style drinks; other fruit syrups like raspberry and peach; and cream of coconut syrups like Coco López, used in a Piña Colada (page 91). All of these, plus many more, can be ordered online or purchased from your favorite cocktail supply shop.

bitters

Bitters are a concentrated solution of spices and other flavors usually steeped in alcohol. They are used only a dash or two at a time in cocktails to enhance flavor, add nuance, and provide balancing bitterness.

An important tool in the bartending arsenal, bitters are essentially the equivalent of something like vanilla extract for baking or salt for cooking—you need only a very small quantity for a whole recipe, but if you leave it out, the thing just won't taste right.

There are a million options out there, all sold in small bottles, but you really need only three for your home bar:

- **angostura aromatic bitters,** which has lovely warm flavors of clove and cinnamon

- **orange bitters** (I like Regan's) to add notes of orange peel as a bright, fresh option

- **peychaud's bitters,** a New Orleans brand that has notes of anise, cherry, and nutmeg

For the recipes in this book, rather than use equal parts of bitters, which would be way too strong, I'll cheat a little bit and tell you to add a couple dashes here and there. As long as you don't go overboard, it's hard to mess up, and a couple of dashes of good bitters will make your drinks way more interesting.

Think of these three ingredients, along with absinthe, as your basic spice rack for cocktails.

absinthe

A couple of recipes in this book, such as the Corpse Reviver #2 (page 74) and the Buckskin Playmate (page 140) also call for absinthe, a traditional French liqueur made with wormwood and aniseed. It has an intense flavor that can be a bit overpowering, so we're going to use only a few drops at a time, the same as you would with bitters. A great brand is Kübler, which is available in small, half-size bottles to save you a bit of money while building your home bar. And don't worry, despite the century-old unfounded claims, it won't make you hallucinate!

Real absinthe was banned in the United States for nearly a hundred years, but it was legalized again in 2007 after folks realized it's perfectly safe. If you can't find real absinthe, you can use Herbsaint, which is like absinthe but without the wormwood, or you can also substitute it with lighter (and cheaper) French aniseed liqueurs called "pastis," the most famous brand being Pernod.

other key cocktail ingredients

There are a handful of other components you'll need to have on hand to make sure your cocktails shine. But don't worry, none of them are expensive or hard to find. A trip to the local supermarket is all you should need to stock up on these basics.

citrus juices

More than half of the drinks in this book call for freshly squeezed lemon or lime juice, so it's always good to have plenty of whole citrus on hand. Avoid bottled juices. Not only will your drinks taste way better, but you can also use the peels of the whole fruit as aromatic garnishes. For other citrus juices, like orange and grapefruit juice, it's okay to use bottled versions as long as they're 100 percent juice (not from concentrate!), but freshly squeezed will always be better.

other fruit juices

Many cocktails call for other kinds of juice like pineapple juice, apple juice, or cranberry juice. For these, it's fine to use commercial bottled versions—just make sure they're made from real fruit and not fake flavoring.

soda and other mixers

You'll also want to have a few basic mixers on hand like soda water, tonic water, Coca-Cola, ginger beer, and sparkling wine. These are great for making tall, refreshing drinks like the Long Island Iced Tea (page 104) and the Aperol Spritz (page 54).

egg whites

Raw egg whites, the clear part of an egg that can be separated from the yolk, are the traditional way to give cocktails like whiskey sours the frothy and fluffy texture that sets them apart. Egg whites are generally safe to consume raw, as long as they're fresh. But if you're vegan, allergic to eggs, nervous about eating raw eggs, or just don't want to be bothered with the mess, there are plenty of alternatives.

Many places sell containers of pasteurized egg whites, often frozen, that are free from bacteria and are more convenient because you don't have to crack and separate the eggs yourself. There are also commercial alternatives like Wonderfoam or Fee Brothers Fee Foam, which are both vegan and can be added to cocktails just a few dashes at a time to achieve nearly the same texture that egg white offers. The liquid from canned chickpeas, known as aquafaba, also works as a 1:1 replacement for egg white in cocktails; it'll just give your drink a slightly salty taste (which I kind of like).

And if you don't want to deal at all with the egg white—real or vegan— any cocktail that calls for it will taste just fine if you leave it out; it just won't have that fluffy texture.

garnishes

The garnish is an important part of most cocktails, both to help them look visually appealing and often to add aromas that elevate the drinking experience, because we always see and smell things before we taste them.

citrus peel

Fresh citrus peels make wonderful garnishes for all sorts of cocktails and reduce waste by using something you'd otherwise throw away. Any kind of citrus peel will make a good garnish because of the aromatic oils contained in citrus skin, but the most common are lemon and orange.

Lemon peel has a light and bright aroma, perfect for more refreshing, less savory martinis, and for lifting the overall experience of heavier drinks to make them a bit more vibrant. Try a lemon peel on a Manhattan (page 56) to brighten it up, for example.

Orange peel has a sweeter, richer aroma, perfect for whiskey, aged tequila, brandy, and dark rum drinks like the Mai Tai (page 60), but it can also add a layer of richness to refreshing drinks like the Cosmopolitan (page 95).

Grapefruit peel has a nice bittersweet aroma that works great with tequila and gin, as in the Semper Fizz (page 147).

To make a citrus peel garnish, cut a wide strip of skin from the fruit with a sharp vegetable peeler or cut it carefully with a sharp paring knife. If using

a knife, you might also have to cut some of the white pith from the inside of the peel by laying it white-side up on a cutting board and using the knife to carefully slice the pith from the peel.

fresh fruit

Fresh fruit works wonderfully as a cocktail garnish as well. You might want to use a wedge of pineapple to garnish a Piña Colada (page 91), for example, or a fresh strawberry for a Frozen Strawberry Daiquiri (page 107). Wedges or circles of citrus or a few slices of apple arranged into a fan are also beautiful and easy.

You can also use leftover bits of fruit to make great garnishes. For example, a couple of pineapple leaves sticking out of a tropical drink looks great, or the skin of half a passion fruit that's been scooped out can float on the top of a drink like a little purple boat.

For smaller berries, or for anything you want to be a little more stable on the rim of your glass, stick them onto a cocktail skewer or toothpick to help them balance on top of your cocktail.

preserved fruit

Preserved fruits like maraschino cherries are one of the most common cocktail garnishes. I'm not a big fan of the cheap, bright red ones you get in most dive bars, so I generally opt for a nice brand, like Luxardo. There are plenty of high-quality ones on the market these days, or you can get crafty and make your own.

Other common preserved fruits that are easy to use include dehydrated citrus and candied ginger. If you have a food dehydrator, you can make these types of things yourself, but they're also readily available at supermarkets.

fresh herbs

Sprigs of fresh, aromatic herbs like mint, rosemary, thyme, and sage are some of the very best garnishes for cocktails because they look beautiful and smell amazing. They're also easy to grow even if you don't have a lot of space.

olives and pickled onions

For martinis, olives are the most popular garnish. Make sure you get olives in brine, not oil, as the oily ones will leave a slick across the top of your drink. You can also use a bit of the brine to make your martini dirty. I prefer the big, bright green Sicilian olives for my martinis, because they have a mild taste and a beautiful color, but you should use whatever you like eating most. You can also find olives stuffed with blue cheese or anchovies for something a little more fancy, or try stuffing olives yourself for a personal touch.

I also love drinking martinis with pickled cocktail onions. They're a little brighter and less salty than olives and are available at most supermarkets.

bottles in this book

Now that you know all the components that go into a well-stocked bar, here's a basic template for the bottles you need to make the recipes in this book, customized for each chapter. Of course, it's important to remember to stock your bar with the things you like! If you love tequila but hate Scotch whisky, well, you can replace the whisky with extra bottles of different tequila and mezcal, and vice versa. These are just suggestions, so don't feel like you have to buy everything listed here to get started.

the all-time greats

Here's what you need to get started making cocktails at home with the classic recipes in this book (pages 46–67), plus many, many others. If you want to drink like the movie stars of old and lock down the world's most famous and long-standing drinks, bottles of these are a must!

- **critical spirits:** gin, rye whiskey or bourbon, Cognac, blanco tequila, Scotch whisky, white rum, and dark rum

- **critical flavor makers:** Campari, sweet vermouth, dry vermouth, off-dry vermouth, Angostura bitters, Drambuie (or other sweet, herbal liqueur such as Bénédictine D.O.M. or Glayva), Cointreau (or other orange liqueur/triple sec), amaretto, and Aperol

- **good to have, but not critical:** mezcal joven, agricole rum or cachaça, Cynar amaro, dry sherry, orange bitters, vodka, Peychaud's bitters, and absinthe (or other aniseed-flavored liqueur such as Herbsaint or Pernod pastis)

forgotten classics

If you want to dive a little deeper and get into the forgotten classics that bartenders are rediscovering (pages 68–87), keep all the above, and add these important ingredients: Irish whiskey, apricot liqueur, peach liqueur, crème de cassis, Heering cherry liqueur, Chartreuse, maraschino liqueur, sloe gin, and grenadine.

drinks just wanna have fun

If you want to keep your bar fun, fresh, and fruity (pages 88–109) and you're less interested in boozy classics like martinis and negronis, here's where you should start:

- **critical spirits:** vodka, Cognac, gin, blanco tequila, dark rum, and white rum
- **critical flavor makers:** coffee liqueur (like Kahlúa), triple sec (like Cointreau), Midori, Coco López (or other sweetened cream of coconut), dry vermouth, Chambord (or other dark berry liqueur), passion fruit liqueur or syrup, strawberry liqueur or syrup, white crème de cacao (or other chocolate liqueur), and Galliano L'Autentico (or other light, herbal liqueur such as Strega or Yellow Chartreuse)

modern classics

For jumping into the world of modern classics (pages 110–131), add these ingredients to the base ingredients you'll need for the All-Time Greats and Forgotten Classics sections: Amaro Nonino, navy-strength gin, Yellow Chartreuse, Islay single-malt Scotch, Gran Classico Bitter, blackstrap rum, cream sherry, ginger liqueur, Suze (or other gentian liqueur), and, if you don't already have mezcal and dry sherry (such as fino), they will be important for this chapter.

wonders of the world

For some of the more advanced modern cocktails in the last chapter (pages 132–151), you'll want to add these to the basics you've built up from previous chapters: red wine, barrel-proof rye whiskey, barrel-proof bourbon, añejo tequila, contemporary gin, pisco, Amaro Montenegro, pineapple rum, St-Germain (or other elderflower liqueur), Rainwater Madeira, Fernet-Branca (or other alpine amaro), Frangelico hazelnut liqueur, Tempus Fugit crème de banane, falernum, and imo shōchū.

the
all-time
greats

Some cocktails are classics for a reason. A true classic should be simple, delicious, easy to replicate, and even easier to drink. All great cocktails should come with a great name and a great story, evoking something intangible that's far more than just cold liquor in a glass.

This section covers ten of the most famous cocktails ever created—the ones that everyone has heard of, even if they've never tried them, because the drinks have developed a cultural identity within the collective unconscious. From cocktails synonymous with class and sophistication enjoyed by movie stars and captains of industry, to tropical libations that send us on a holiday for the senses, these drinks are both timeless and borderless, ordered across decades and across oceans at bars all over the world.

Incredibly simple in their construction and using easy-to-find ingredients, these recipes are a great place to start honing your skills as a home mixologist and learning the basics of cocktail creation.

Any good bartender should know these ten classic cocktail recipes by heart and be able to make them using pure muscle memory. But simplicity can be deceiving, leaving a wide berth for interpretation. The perfect way to make a martini or a Mai Tai is hotly debated among professionals, and also tends to change with trends and availability of ingredients. Here, I'll show you the best way I know based on years of preparing drinks for a living, but once you've done it my way, feel free to experiment to figure out your own. Each bartender's interpretation of the classics is part of their signature style, so find yours and be proud of it.

If you can get these drinks right, you'll be everyone's favorite host or party guest. Who doesn't want someone to offer them a martini before dinner or a mojito as they arrive at the pool party? From swanky soirées to beach-house bacchanalia to a simple after-work drink to ease you into your evening, these classic cocktail recipes will give you the foundation you need to mix delicious drinks for any occasion.

rusty nail

scotch whisky
1 ounce

drambuie
1 ounce

TECHNIQUE
build

GLASS
rocks

The Old Fashioned is one of those simple drinks that's hard to perfect. With just four ingredients—whiskey, sugar, bitters, and ice—it should be a breeze, but the thing about such basic drinks is that there's nowhere to hide. Unless you really nail the proportions, it can be way out of whack. So how to make it foolproof? The Rusty Nail. The Drambuie in this recipe takes the place of both the sugar and the bitters in an Old Fashioned by adding balanced sweetness and spice. Et voilà, the world's easiest whisky cocktail.

Add all of the ingredients directly to the rocks glass, then fill the glass with ice.

Give it a quick stir and garnish with a twist of **orange peel.**

MESS WITH YOUR DRINK
Don't like Scotch or don't have any on hand? Use bourbon, rye, Irish whiskey, Canadian rye whisky, whatever. It'll also work with other dark spirits like dark rum, añejo tequila, and Cognac. If you don't have Drambuie, try other sweet, herbal liqueurs like Bénédictine D.O.M. or Glayva, or even Fireball Cinnamon Whisky or Wild Turkey American Honey (which will work best paired with bourbon or rye).

VARIATION: THE GODFATHER
Try this recipe with equal parts **bourbon** and **amaretto** to create this variation, named after what many consider the greatest movie ever made.

ADVANCED VARIATION: THE VIEUX CARRÉ
This is a classic variation of the Old Fashioned hailing from New Orleans, which many consider to be the birthplace of the cocktail. Rich, complex, and absolutely delicious, this will impress any cocktail aficionado. In a mixing glass, pour equal parts **rye whiskey, Cognac, sweet vermouth, and Bénédictine D.O.M.,** plus a dash of **absinthe** and a dash of **Peychaud's bitters.** Stir with ice, then strain into a chilled rocks glass over a large chunk of ice, and garnish with a twist of **lemon peel.**

martini

dry **boozy** **aromatic**

gin or vodka

1½ ounces

off-dry vermouth

1½ ounces

orange bitters

2 dashes

TECHNIQUE
stir

GLASS
cocktail

No cocktail in the world evokes sophistication quite like the martini. And we're talking about the *real* martini—the one made with gin (or vodka) and a bit of vermouth, served ice cold and garnished with an olive that gazes at you seductively through the haze of a perfectly chilled martini glass. This is not a drink for people who like sweet things or who don't like the taste of alcohol. That's part of why it's considered such a sophisticated cocktail—it's not for amateur drinkers. A good martini is savory and dry, with no juice or soda or anything to hide the punchiness of the liquor. Most martinis are made with about five parts gin or vodka to one part vermouth, and some have even less vermouth than that. But these days, vermouth-heavy martinis are coming back into style in a big way. Enter the equal parts martini, a super-simple recipe that results in a complex, delicious cocktail that's smoother than Clark Gable in a tuxedo.

Add all of the ingredients to a mixing glass, fill with ice, and stir until the outside of the glass starts to feel cold.

Strain into a chilled cocktail glass and garnish with an **olive,** a **cocktail onion,** or for something more refreshing, a twist of **lemon peel.**

VARIATION: DIRTY MARTINI
Exactly the same as above, but with 1 ounce of cold **olive brine** added to the mix.

MAKE IT FOR COMPANY
Take a whole bottle each of **vermouth** and **gin,** mix them together in a large container with ½ ounce of **orange bitters,** then decant the liquid back into the bottles and keep them in the freezer. When company arrives, or when you get a hankering for a martini, just pop open the bottle and, voilà, perfectly chilled and ready to pour.

ADVANCED VARIATION:
THE JABBERWOCKY
My favorite variation is called the Jabberwocky, named after the Louis Carroll poem, and was first published in *The Savoy Cocktail Book* (1930). Use 1 ounce **gin,** 1 ounce **off-dry vermouth,** 1 ounce **dry sherry** (I like fino), plus 2 dashes of **orange bitters,** prepared as above and garnished with a twist of **lemon peel** or, if they're in season, **red grapefruit peel.**

negroni

bittersweet · **aromatic** · **boozy**

gin
1 ounce

campari
1 ounce

sweet vermouth
1 ounce

TECHNIQUE
build

GLASS
rocks

The simple combination of gin, Campari, and sweet vermouth has been a worldwide favorite for more than a hundred years, and it's one of the very first cocktails most bartenders learn how to make. If you've never had one before, it might take a little getting used to, as the bitterness of Campari paired with herbal vermouth and savory gin make this a decidedly adult drink. But if you like your cocktails with plenty of booze and not too sweet, this is the one for you. It's also one of the easiest cocktails to make at home, requiring no fresh ingredients and very little technique.

Add all of the ingredients directly to the rocks glass, then fill the glass with ice.

Give it a quick stir and garnish with a twist of **orange peel.**

MESS WITH YOUR DRINK
One of the great things about this drink is that it's super easy to modify it to your own tastes. If you find the Campari a little intense, for example, replace it with less-bitter Aperol. Don't like gin? Just about any spirit will work in its place. My favorite is tequila or mezcal, but whiskey is great, too. Want it brighter and even less sweet? Try using an off-dry vermouth instead of sweet vermouth.

VARIATION: NEGRONI SBAGLIATO
This version of the Negroni set the internet on fire when it was mentioned in an interview with *House of the Dragon* stars Olivia Cooke and Emma D'Arcy. For this version, replace the gin with **sparkling wine** and serve it in a wineglass like a spritz. *Sbagliato* means *mistaken* in Italian, but I think this mistaken Negroni is spot-on when the sun's out.

aperol spritz

aperol
2 ounces

sparkling wine
2 ounces

soda water
2 ounces

TECHNIQUE
build

GLASS
large wineglass

The Aperol Spritz is one of the most crowd-pleasing cocktails ever created. And it's incredibly easy to prepare—no shaking or specialized equipment of any kind required. It's also perfect to make in big batches for a group of people, and easy to modify to your own tastes and the ingredients you have on hand. Spritzes are also lower in alcohol than most cocktails, so you can have more than one without getting sloppy.

Add all of the ingredients directly to the wineglass, give it a quick stir, then fill the glass with ice and garnish with a wedge of **orange** and an **olive.**

Add a straw if you don't want to leave lipstick on the glass. And if you want this to look like something out of a luxury lifestyle magazine, add a sprig of fresh herbs like **mint, thyme,** or **rosemary.**

MESS WITH YOUR DRINK
If you prefer something with a little more richness and bitterness, this drink works perfectly with Campari instead of Aperol or really any other amaro you enjoy. The basic spritz formula of liquor + sparkling wine + soda also works great with vermouths and sherries for drier versions, and with fruit or floral spirits like Chambord black raspberry liqueur or St-Germain elderflower liqueur if you prefer things a little sweeter, making the spritz wonderfully refreshing and super-flexible sunny-day sipping no matter what you have on hand.

MAKE IT FOR COMPANY
In a large pitcher, add 2 cups of **Aperol,** 2 cups of **sparkling wine,** and 2 cups of **soda water,** then fill with ice and stir. Garnish with a few slices of **orange** and pour into wineglasses to serve.

manhattan

rye whiskey
1 ounce

cognac
1 ounce

sweet vermouth
1 ounce

cynar amaro
1 ounce

TECHNIQUE
stir

GLASS
cocktail

Dryer and more complex than an Old Fashioned, the Manhattan works just as well as an apéritif as it does after dinner. Traditionally, a Manhattan is made with two parts of rye whiskey to one part of sweet vermouth, with a couple of dashes of Angostura bitters. And while this iconic cocktail is one of the most riffed on and modified out there, this simple combination has survived nearly unchanged from its original formula for close to 150 years. My equal parts version of the Manhattan, which my colleague John Hallett helped me develop, includes Cognac for additional depth and complexity, as well as earthy, savory Cynar amaro.

Add everything to a mixing glass with ice.

Stir until chilled, then strain into a chilled cocktail glass and garnish with a twist of **lemon** or, if you prefer, a **maraschino cherry.**

MESS WITH YOUR DRINK
This recipe will also work if you want to keep it simple by eliminating the Cognac and doubling the rye, or you can play around by replacing the Cognac with another kind of aged brandy, like applejack, or even something like añejo tequila. Bourbon or Scotch will also work fine instead of the rye.

VARIATION: THE SUPER-SIMPLE VERSION
Use equal parts **rye whiskey** and **sweet vermouth** with a couple of dashes of **Angostura bitters.** This will give you a rich, sweet Manhattan. If you prefer things a little more bitter, try equal parts **rye whiskey** and **Cynar amaro** instead.

the origins of the manhattan

There are few drinks that evoke sophistication like the Manhattan, in large part because of its origin as a true New York City classic. The story goes that the drink was invented at New York's Manhattan Club in 1874 for a party thrown by socialite Jennie Jerome celebrating the election of Samuel J. Tilden as the state's governor. But this story is exceedingly unlikely, as the election was held on November 3, and Jennie Jerome's first son, Winston (who would go on to become England's most famous prime minister), was born on November 30 at Blenheim Place, Oxfordshire, England, making it hard to believe that Jennie was in New York downing whiskey cocktails, heavily pregnant, less than a month earlier.

Apocryphal stories about the origin of the Manhattan aside, by 1882 there were written references to the drink in a syndicated newspaper column of New York City gossip. The column states, "It is but a short time ago that a mixture of whiskey, vermouth, and bitters came into vogue" and remarks that it had been known as a Turf Club cocktail, a Jockey Club cocktail, and a Manhattan cocktail. So, at the very least, we know the drink comes from New York City and was probably first mixed in the late 1870s or early 1880s.

It's worth noting that this was a time when a lot of Italians were arriving in New York City, bringing with them their favorite fortified wine, vermouth. This gave rise to cocktails like the martini (named after the famous Italian brand of vermouth) and the Manhattan. So thank you, Italian Americans!

mojito

white rum

1 ounce

off-dry vermouth

1 ounce

lime juice

1 ounce

simple syrup

1 ounce

mint leaves

a good handful

soda water

to top

TECHNIQUE
shake

GLASS
highball

The Mojito is a Cuban invention that became globally popular during Prohibition (1920–1933), when Americans who could afford the trip flocked to Havana in droves to party and drink. Employing the fundamental cocktail trinity of booze, sour, and sweet (rum, lime, and sugar in this case), the Mojito is made even more refreshing with the addition of soda water and fresh mint. One of the primary establishments in 1920s Havana serving Mojitos to spirits-starved Yankees was Sloppy Joe's. The recipe below is my version of their special "Caballito" Mojito.

Add everything except the soda water to a cocktail shaker with ice.

Shake hard for 10 seconds or so, until the outside of the shaker starts to get frosty.

Pour the entire contents of the shaker, ice and all, without straining into the highball glass.

Top with soda water, give it a quick stir, and garnish with a sprig of **mint.**

MESS WITH YOUR DRINK
If you want to make a more traditional Mojito, eliminate the vermouth and double the white rum. If this recipe is a little too sweet for your liking, reduce the simple syrup a little, and if it comes out too sour, reduce the lime juice. You can also easily turn your mojito into a cucumber Mojito by adding a few small chunks of fresh cucumber directly to the shaker with everything else for a refreshing, savory kick.

MAKE IT FOR COMPANY
In a pitcher that can hold at least 48 ounces, add 1 cup each of **rum, lime juice, vermouth,** and **simple syrup,** then chill in the refrigerator. When it's time to serve, add a bunch of **mint leaves** and top the pitcher up with **soda water,** then give it a stir. To serve, pour it out into tall glasses filled with ice for each of your guests and garnish each glass with a sprig of **mint** or a slice of **cucumber.**

mai tai

rich **tropical** **complex**

jamaican dark rum
¾ ounce

agricole rum
or cachaça
¾ ounce

cointreau or other
orange liqueur/
triple sec
¾ ounce

lime juice
¾ ounce

amaretto
¾ ounce

TECHNIQUE
shake

GLASS
rocks

The Mai Tai is my all-time favorite cocktail. Nothing says "tropical vacation" more than a sweet, icy rum drink, and to me the Mai Tai is the epitome of tropical cocktails. Many of the most famous tropical drinks have been badly bastardized over the years, ending up as syrupy fruit bombs packed with artificial flavor and poor-quality spirits. The best thing about the Mai Tai is that when made right, it maintains all the subtlety and nuance of the best classics, while still ticking the tropical fun box in a big way.

Add all of the ingredients to a cocktail shaker with ice.

Shake hard for 10 seconds or so, until the outside of the shaker starts to get frosty.

Strain into a chilled rocks glass and fill with crushed ice. (Alternatively, you can simply dump the entire contents of the shaker without straining into the glass for a sort of slushy effect.)

Garnish with a wedge of **orange,** a **preserved cherry,** a sprig of **mint,** and a paper cocktail umbrella.

MESS WITH YOUR DRINK
If you don't have two kinds of rum on hand, that's fine. Just use one and double the amount. You can also use orgeat, an almond syrup you can buy from cocktail supply stores, instead of amaretto, but it will be sweeter, so use a little less, maybe ¼ to ½ ounce.

PRO TIP: ORANGE LIQUEUR
Orange-flavored liqueur, also referred to as "triple sec" or "Curaçao," is a critical ingredient in countless cocktails. The most common brand found in bars is Cointreau, and it's perfect for every recipe in this book that calls for orange liqueur. Pierre Ferrand dry Curaçao is also a favorite among professional bartenders.

the origins
of the mai tai

The balance and complexity of the Mai Tai make sense given the drink's origins. It was invented by Victor "Trader Vic" Bergeron, a classically trained chef and restaurateur who became one of the most influential characters in the mid-twentieth-century American cultural phenomenon called Tropicana. Spanning everything from movies and music to fashion, architecture, and food, tropical mania hit the United States hard during the post–World War II boom. The middle class was growing, and the way Americans were spending their leisure time was changing.

All of a sudden, middle-class folks could afford to travel by air or cruise ship to places like Hawaii and the Caribbean. But if that was out of budget, they could simply hop in their Studebaker and head to a local tropical-themed venue for a fruity rum drink and a pu pu platter surrounded by bamboo and giant clam shells.

Trader Vic copied the original master of tropical rum drinks in the U.S., Donn "Don the Beachcomber" Beach (creator of classics like the Zombie and Missionary's Downfall), but made his cocktails less complicated while maintaining all the fun and escapism. And while Don kept his cocktail formulas jealously guarded secrets, Vic published multiple recipe books, helping drinks like the Mai Tai gain international recognition.

The story goes that while making cocktails for friends at his restaurant in Oakland, Vic tried out a combination of Jamaican rum, Curaçao, lime juice, and almond syrup. Upon sipping this new combination, they exclaimed, "Mai tai!"—a Tahitian colloquialism for "very good"—and the Mai Tai was born.

sidecar

citrusy   **rich**   **punchy**

cognac
1½ ounces

cointreau or other orange liqueur/triple sec
1½ ounces

lemon juice
1½ ounces

TECHNIQUE
shake

GLASS
cocktail

The last time I was in Paris, I had what I consider to be one of the fundamental cocktail experiences: a Sidecar at Harry's New York Bar. This simple drink of brandy, triple sec, and lemon juice represents a seismic shift in cocktail history brought on by Prohibition. During the 1920s, American bartenders left the country in droves as their trade was made illegal overnight. Thus, the American cocktail went international, with American-style cocktail bars opening up all over the world. One such bar was Harry's in Paris, a joint owned by Scottish bartender Harry MacElhone, who had worked in New York, and a place that's remained largely unchanged for a hundred years. This, it is said, is where the Sidecar was invented, and it's a drink that has stood the test of time. Rich and refreshing in equal parts (pun intended), the Sidecar is one of those cocktails that sits perfectly between the brighter, fresher drinks of the daytime and the richer, stronger drinks of the night; a twilight cocktail, if you will.

Add everything to a cocktail shaker with ice.

Shake hard for 10 seconds or so, until the outside of the shaker starts to get frosty.

Fine strain into a chilled cocktail glass, no garnish required.

MESS WITH YOUR DRINK
Many people like to garnish a Sidecar by rimming the glass with granulated sugar. I don't find it necessary with this drink as it's sweet enough without the sugar, but it does look pretty, so for a bit of extra flair, you can do this by wiping a slice of fresh lemon around the outside of the glass to moisten it, then gently rotating the outside of the rim into a dish of sugar and shaking off the excess.

margarita

blanco tequila (unaged)

1 ounce

mezcal joven (unaged)

1 ounce

cointreau or other orange liqueur/triple sec

1 ounce

lime juice

1 ounce

pineapple juice

1 ounce

TECHNIQUE
shake

GLASS
cocktail

At its most basic level, a margarita is made with tequila, orange liqueur, and fresh lime juice. There are a million variations, from the frozen kind made with store-bought margarita mix to high-end craft versions with esoteric formulas. Here, we're taking an in-between approach that works nicely with an equal parts formula—more complex than a standard margarita, but still super easy to remember and make. The inclusion of mezcal, tequila's older, more robust sibling, will introduce elements of smoke and earthiness to the drink to really give it some power. But if you want to keep it simple or you don't have mezcal on hand, just remove the mezcal and double the tequila.

Add everything to a cocktail shaker with ice.

Shake hard for 10 seconds or so, until the outside of the shaker starts to get frosty.

Fine strain into a chilled cocktail glass rimmed with **kosher salt** and garnish with a **lime wheel.**

PRO TIP: SALT RIM
To rim your glass with salt for a proper margarita, first pour some salt onto a small plate—flaky salt like kosher or sea salt flakes will look and taste best! Take a slice of lime and wipe it around the outside rim of your empty glass to moisten it. Gently dip the outside of the glass sideways into the salt; don't jam it in upside down! Lift the glass, rotate, and dip again as many times as you need to cover the whole rim. If you get some salt on the inside of the glass, hold it upside down and wipe out the inside with a napkin to avoid getting salt in the drink itself.

super-simple frozen margarita

blanco tequila

10 ounces

margarita mix
(the jose cuervo brand is pretty good)

10 ounces

lime juice

as much as you can get from 1 lime

angostura bitters

10 dashes

ice

5 cups

TECHNIQUE
blend

GLASS
margarita coupette

The margarita recipe on page 65 will work well for frozen margaritas; just add the ingredients to a blender with plenty of ice and let 'er rip. But sometimes you just want a big frothy jug of frozen marg, and you can't be bothered with squeezing all those fresh limes. I get it. If I'm sitting by the pool on a hot day, I'm actually a sucker for a sugary frozen margarita made with store-bought margarita mix—artificial flavor, green food coloring, and high-fructose corn syrup galore. So here's how I do it. The bitters and fresh lime here will give just enough balance and complexity to your frozen margaritas that your guests will think you did the whole thing from scratch. This recipe makes enough cocktail for about five servings.

Add everything to a blender.

Blend until slushy in texture. Pour into margarita glasses rimmed with **kosher salt** (see the Pro Tip on page 65).

amaretto sour

sweet   **frothy**   **nutty**

amaretto

1 ounce

scotch whisky

1 ounce

lemon juice

1 ounce

egg white
*(see page 41 for
alternatives)*

1 ounce

TECHNIQUE
shake

GLASS
rocks

This drink is a perennial favorite; sweet, sour, frothy, and delicious, it has all the sophistication of a proper cocktail while still being super easy to drink. The traditional sour recipe would call for two parts of amaretto to one part lemon juice, but I like to prepare mine a little differently, adding Scotch whisky along with the amaretto to make it more complex and a little less sweet.

Add everything to a cocktail shaker with ice.

Shake hard for 10 seconds or so, until the outside of the shaker starts to get frosty.

Fine strain into a chilled rocks glass, fill with ice, and garnish with a twist of **lemon peel.**

MESS WITH YOUR DRINK
This formula also works well with rye whiskey, bourbon, brandy, or aged tequila instead of Scotch if you don't have any on hand. You could even use vodka if you want to keep it nice and light. To make this drink the traditional way, just eliminate the Scotch and double the amaretto. The same basic formula will also work for whisky sours and pisco sours, too.

VARIATION: AMARETTO CAMPARI SOUR
To really kick it up a notch, some bartenders are now adding Campari to their Amaretto Sours for a modern take on the classic. The result is bittersweet and refreshing but still true to its Italian identity. The other advantage is that the Campari will froth up without the need for egg white; just make the above drink with equal parts **amaretto, Campari,** and fresh **lemon juice.**

forgotten classics

68

During Prohibition, the vast majority of classic cocktails faded from the collective consciousness of American drinkers. Only the most famous drinks, like the ones covered in the previous chapter, remained. These days, people are far more likely to recognize modern drinks like the Espresso Martini and the Cosmo than they are the daisies, slings, toddies, and bucks that were famous among the tipplers of the pre-Prohibition era.

But for those of us who work as professional bartenders in this incredible age of cocktail revival, these forgotten classics offer a framework for creating modern cocktails with a solid grounding in the work of the past. Like Renaissance scholars relearning the works of ancient Greek and Roman philosophers, we pour over the dusty tomes of cocktail history, seeking the best ingredients, the best techniques, and the best formulas for making mixology relevant once more, pushing the craft to new heights of creativity and deliciousness.

The following ten recipes are some of my favorite classic cocktails—ones I've made and consumed countless times because they're easy to remember, easy to make, taste brilliant, and are still appealing to modern tastes. Every good bartender has a few drinks like these up their sleeve so they can whip something up for any guest and occasion, from the bright and fresh to the fun and fruity to the serious and boozy. I've selected cocktails for this chapter with that in mind, providing a great base of delicious recipes from which to build your cocktail knowledge, and all fit perfectly into the equal parts formula.

aprico secco

gin
1 ounce

dry vermouth
1 ounce

apricot liqueur
1 ounce

TECHNIQUE
stir

GLASS
cocktail

The Aprico Secco (Italian for *dry apricot*) is essentially an apricot-flavored martini. It has the basic building blocks of a martini—gin and dry vermouth—but also includes apricot liqueur for a sweet/tart hit of fruitiness. A great option if two shots of cold gin in a classic martini is a bit more than you can handle, this drink also bridges the gap between savory, dry martinis and the fruity, shaken martinis of the 1990s era, like appletinis and lychee martinis. It's not nearly as dry as the classic but is better balanced and closer to it than those fruity guys, which are really fruit sours more than martinis. This recipe appears in the hugely influential *Savoy Cocktail Book* by Harry Craddock, published in 1930. Thanks to my friend and colleague Nathan Beasley for introducing me to this drink.

Add everything to a mixing glass and fill with ice.

Stir until the outside of the glass starts to feel cold.

Strain into a chilled cocktail glass and garnish with a twist of **lemon peel.**

charlie chaplin

sweet **fruity** **frothy**

sloe gin
1 ounce

apricot liqueur
1 ounce

lime juice
1 ounce

TECHNIQUE
shake

GLASS
cocktail

This wonderful classic, named after the famed silent movie actor, has always been a standard for bartenders. If someone asks you for something sweet and fruity, but you don't have any fresh fruit on hand and you want to stick with a tried-and-true recipe, this is the perfect solution. The use of sloe gin helps as well. Sloe gin is a traditional style of gin sweetened and infused with sloeberries, the fruit of the blackthorn tree, offering the complexity of gin with the sweetness of fresh berries. In my early days of bartending at classic cocktail bars, the Charlie Chaplin was also my go-to shooter to prepare for guests. This was a time when a lot of Australians weren't accustomed to American cocktails, but they *loved* fruity mixed shots like the Kamikaze. So rather than saying "We don't do that here" when someone asked for a round of shooters, I'd mix up a Charlie Chaplin and pour it out into shot glasses. I'd then regale them with the story of the drink and use it as a chance to get people excited about classic cocktails.

Add everything to a cocktail shaker with ice.

Shake hard for 10 seconds or so, until the outside of the shaker starts to get frosty.

Fine strain into a chilled cocktail glass and garnish with a twist of **lime peel.**

VARIATION: THE MILLIONAIRE
For something a little sweeter, add 1 ounce of **grenadine** to the formula above. Grenadine is a pomegranate syrup that's great for making cocktails, the most famous being a Tequila Sunrise. It's worth spending a few extra bucks on a good-quality bottle, as the cheap ones you find in dive bars are full of fake flavors and coloring.

corpse reviver #2

refreshing **complex** **sour**

gin
1 ounce

off-dry vermouth
1 ounce

lemon juice
1 ounce

cointreau or other orange liqueur/triple sec
1 ounce

absinthe
1 barspoon

TECHNIQUE
shake

GLASS
cocktail

In the pre-Prohibition era, the booze-twisted psyche of drinkers and the bartenders who served them created a whole class of "corpse reviver" cocktails as hangover cures. The idea behind these drinks is that they're sour and bracing enough to toss back quickly without upsetting the delicate constitution of the hungover customer, while also containing enough booze to offer the old "hair of the dog" effect. This particular recipe is fundamental for any professional cocktail bartender, and often one of the first ones we learn. Easy to remember, sporting a wonderfully memorable name, and perfect if you like your drinks on the dryer, more sour side, it's one of those cocktails that has survived for more than 150 years for good reason.

Add everything to a cocktail shaker with ice.

Shake hard for 10 seconds or so, until the outside of the shaker starts to get frosty.

Fine strain into a chilled cocktail glass and garnish with a twist of **lemon peel.**

VARIATION: TWENTIETH CENTURY
This drink appears in William J. Tarling's 1937 *Café Royal Cocktail Book,* credited to British bartender C. A. Tuck. Replace the orange liqueur with a **white chocolate liqueur,** commonly known as "white crème de cacao," and don't include the absinthe.

This version is sweeter than a Corpse Reviver. Something nutty like **amaretto** (almond liqueur) or **Frangelico** (hazelnut liqueur) would also work if you want a drink that's a little sweeter and richer. Just avoid any spirits that are dark or creamy, as that will turn your drink into a muddy mess!

what the hell is off-dry vermouth?

This is an ingredient that's so important to the equal parts formula that it's worth taking a closer look. Off-dry vermouth, like dry vermouth, is an aromatized white wine. That means it's a white wine that's been infused with various herbs and spices, at least one of them offering a bit of bitterness, as well as some extra alcohol to help preserve it. But off-dry vermouth also has a little extra sugar added, giving it more sweetness and palate weight than its dry sibling, while still not nearly as rich and powerful as sweet vermouth (which is made with red wine, more sugar, and richer flavorings). Sweet vermouth would be overpowering in a drink like the Corpse Reviver, while dry vermouth could throw off the balance in the other direction, making the drink not sweet enough.

For a brand of aromatized wine that will work for every recipe in this book that calls for off-dry vermouth, try Lillet Blanc or Cocchi Americano. They're also delicious to drink on the rocks with a slice of pink grapefruit, or as a refreshing and low-alcohol spritz with soda water and a bit of sparkling wine.

old pal

rye whiskey or bourbon
1 ounce

dry vermouth
1 ounce

campari
1 ounce

TECHNIQUE
stir

GLASS
cocktail

The Old Pal is somewhere in between a Negroni and a Manhattan, but the inclusion of dry vermouth instead of sweet makes it less sweet than either of its equal parts relatives. I like to think of the Old Pal as a Manhattan for before dinner, when you don't want too much richness or sugar to ruin your palate for the meal to come. This is yet another classic that comes to us from Harry MacElhone, this time from the 1952 edition of *Harry's ABC of Mixing Drinks.* As with many of these simple equal parts cocktails, the base spirit can be whatever you like or whatever you have on hand. Aged rum, aged tequila, brandy, or whatever whiskey you have on hand will work just fine for this recipe, as long as it's something you like to drink!

Add everything to a mixing glass, then fill with ice.

Stir until the outside of the mixing glass starts to feel cold.

Strain into a chilled cocktail glass and garnish with a twist of **orange peel.**

VARIATION: BOULEVARDIER
The Boulevardier is even closer to a classic Negroni as it uses **bourbon (or rye whiskey)** in equal parts with **Campari** and **sweet vermouth,** so basically a Negroni with bourbon instead of gin. See how easy it is to mess around with these recipes to create something different?

the last word

bright **complex** **aromatic**

gin
1 ounce

lime juice
1 ounce

maraschino liqueur
1 ounce

chartreuse
1 ounce

TECHNIQUE
shake

GLASS
cocktail

The Last Word is one of the first classic equal parts cocktails that most bartenders learn, probably only second to the Negroni. Gin and citrus make it incredibly drinkable, while the complexity and sweetness of Chartreuse are balanced by the dry fruit character of maraschino liqueur for one of those perfect drinks that's much more than the sum of its parts. This recipe employs the basic formula of many modern equal parts cocktails: one part spirit, one part citrus, and then one part each of two other powerfully flavored ingredients. It's a combination that's been riffed on a million times, allowing for endless experimentation. In this case, the result is a drink of huge depth and sophistication while still offering refreshment.

Add everything to a cocktail shaker with ice.

Shake hard for 10 seconds or so, until the outside of the shaker starts to get frosty.

Fine strain into a chilled cocktail glass and garnish with a good **maraschino cherry.**

PRO TIP: GET GOOD CHERRIES!
Quality cocktail cherries are well worth the investment. Try brands like Amarena Fabbri, Luxardo, or Tempus Fugit (all available online or from your local cocktail supply shop). They are more pricy than the fluorescent-red ones, but compared to your other cocktail ingredients, they're an inexpensive addition per drink, and why would you ruin a great cocktail with a crappy garnish?

VARIATION: THE FINAL WARD
The most famous variation on the Last Word comes from Phil Ward, who created this version at Pegu Club in New York back in 2006. Replace the gin with **rye whiskey** and switch out the lime juice for **lemon juice.**

the origins of the last word

The Last Word was created at the Detroit Athletic Club around 1916, just before Prohibition rained destruction down on American cocktail creativity. The drink's popularity was spurred on by Irish-American vaudeville performer Frank Fogarty, known as "The Dublin Minstrel," who visited the club in Detroit and took the recipe for the Last Word back to his hometown of New York. The drink managed somehow to survive Prohibition in the thirsty minds of New York and first appeared in print in *Bottoms Up,* a 1951 cocktail recipe book by Waldorf-Astoria Hotel publicist Ted Saucier.

Despite its inclusion in Saucier's book, the Last Word never really took off as a well-known classic, even among bartenders, until the cocktail revival of the early 2000s, when bars like Seattle's Zig Zag Café and New York's Clover Club put it on their menus. The drink's simple recipe and use of out-of-fashion but still easy-to-find ingredients like maraschino liqueur and Chartreuse made it a hit with bartenders (when we're busy, we always recommend the easy stuff!), and thus the Last Word became a staple for modern mixologists.

fish house punch

complex **refreshing** **juicy**

dark rum
1 ounce

cognac
1 ounce

**peach liqueur
(see tip)**
1 ounce

lemon juice
1 ounce

lime juice
1 ounce

simple syrup
1 ounce

TECHNIQUE
shake

GLASS
highball

During the Colonial era, big bowls of punch filled with multiple different spirits and various citrus juices and spices were all the rage at gentlemen's clubs and high-end taverns. One such place was the Philadelphia Fish House, an angling clubhouse frequented by folks like George Washington himself. The Fish House Punch, scaled down in the recipe below, is a wonderful example of how different spirits and citrus juices can work together to create something much more than the sum of its parts. It is perfect for experimentation with various spirits and liqueurs, so as always, don't be afraid to play around with the components.

Add everything to a cocktail shaker with ice.

Shake hard for 10 seconds or so, until the outside of the shaker starts to get frosty.

Strain into a highball glass, top it up with as much ice as possible, and garnish with a sprig of fresh **mint** and a **lemon wheel.**

PRO TIP: PEACH LIQUEURS
Peach liqueurs are sometimes called "crème de pêche," "peach brandy," or "peach schnapps." Any of these will work for this recipe, but I recommend a high-quality French brand like Massenez or Marie Brizard for classic cocktails.

MAKE IT FOR COMPANY
In a big punch bowl, pour full bottles of the **rum, brandy,** and **peach liqueur.** Then, add the same volume each of **lemon juice, lime juice,** and **simple syrup.** Let it chill in the refrigerator overnight. At the same time, make a big block of ice for the punch by filling a freezer-safe container with water, and allow it to freeze solid in the freezer for at least twenty-four hours. Tip the ice block out of the container and add it to the punch bowl—it will melt very slowly, keeping your punch cool for the whole evening. When serving your punch, you can stretch it out and make it less alcoholic by topping it up with **pineapple juice, soda water,** or **ginger ale.**

el diablo

fizzy **refreshing** **fruity**

tequila
1 ounce

lime juice
1 ounce

**crème de cassis
(see tip)**
1 ounce

ginger beer
to top

TECHNIQUE
shake

GLASS
highball

El Diablo was an all-time favorite during my time behind the bar at the Black Pearl in Melbourne, one of Australia's longest running and most famous cocktail bars. This easy-to-make and delicious cocktail was second only to the Espresso Martini in raw numbers. It employs ginger beer as one of the primary ingredients, a great mixer for nearly any spirit because it offers sweetness, spice, and wonderfully gingery aromatics. El Diablo comes to us from Victor "Trader Vic" Bergeron, that same midcentury mastermind of tropicana who gave us the Mai Tai. The recipe appeared in his 1946 *Trader Vic's Book of Food and Drink.*

Add everything but the ginger beer to a cocktail shaker, then fill with ice.

Shake for just a few seconds to mix the ingredients. (We're going to top this with ginger beer, so you don't need much dilution.)

Strain into a highball glass, fill it with ice, then top up with ginger beer.

Garnish with a **lime wheel.**

PRO TIP: BERRY LIQUEURS
Liqueurs like the crème de cassis are an important tool in the bartender's kit. Unlike syrups, they tend to be a bit more balanced and less sweet and include the lovely brightness and acidity of fresh berries.

Crème de cassis is made from blackcurrants (*cassis* in French), but any dark berry liqueur can be used in this recipe. Crème de mûre is made from blackberries, and is a little sweeter but will work well, as will Chambord, which is made from black raspberries.

scofflaw

rye whiskey

1 ounce

dry vermouth

1 ounce

lemon juice

1 ounce

grenadine

1 ounce

TECHNIQUE
shake

GLASS
cocktail

In 1923, banker and ardent prohibitionist Delcevare King created a national competition offering $200 in solid gold as a prize to anyone who could come up with the best new word to describe a person who continued to drink despite Prohibition. *Scofflaw* was the winning entry, and it's a term still used today to describe someone exhibiting habitual disregard for statute. Within weeks, an American bartender in Paris came up with a cocktail, christened after the new word, to poke fun at Prohibition in the most obvious way he could. It's a delicious drink, refreshing and fruity despite the inclusion of whiskey. At the Kodiak Club, Australia's first dedicated American whiskey bar, we served our Scofflaws out of mini glass Coca-Cola bottles, a nod to the surreptitious nature of drinking cocktails during Prohibition, and to the fact that the banning of alcohol in the United States led to the rise of soda fountains, ushering in the age of the soft drink.

Add everything to a cocktail shaker with ice.

Shake hard for 10 seconds or so, until the outside of the shaker starts to get frosty.

Fine strain into a chilled cocktail glass and garnish with a twist of **lemon peel.** (Or, for the Kodiak Club version, funnel the strained drink into an empty small-format Coke bottle and serve with a straw—the G-men will never know you're drinking hooch!)

cameron's kick

irish whiskey (see tip)

1 ounce

scotch whisky (see tip)

1 ounce

orgeat

1 ounce

lemon juice

1 ounce

TECHNIQUE
shake

GLASS
cocktail

The Cameron's Kick comes from *Harry's ABC of Mixing Cocktails* first published in 1922 by Harry MacElhone, the very same Harry from Harry's New York Bar in Paris where the Sidecar (page 63) was invented. It's another great cocktail for whiskey drinkers who want something with a bit of refreshing citrus. It's also one of the rare classics that combines two kinds of whiskey in a relatively simple formula: Scotch whisky for a punch of richness, counterbalanced with lighter-bodied Irish whiskey. This drink also includes orgeat, one of my favorite ingredients of all time. It's a rich almond syrup that works wonderfully with almost any spirit, but especially with aged spirits like whiskey, rum, and brandy. It can make any simple combination of spirit and citrus really sing.

Add everything to a cocktail shaker with ice.

Shake hard for 10 seconds or so, until the outside of the shaker starts to get frosty.

Fine strain into a chilled cocktail glass and garnish with a twist of **lemon peel.**

PRO TIP: CHOOSING WHISK(E)Y Choosing ingredients for this cocktail can be a bit of a challenge as there's such a wide variety of flavors. For the Irish whiskey in this one, I'd stick with something standard like Jameson or Bushmills, or maybe a Redbreast if you want to get a little more premium and be able to enjoy some of the bottle neat as well. For the Scotch whisky, something nice and malty is going to work well. Monkey Shoulder is a great option, or Dalwhinnie single malt if you want to splurge.

blood and sand

scotch whisky
1 ounce

heering cherry liqueur
1 ounce

sweet vermouth
1 ounce

grapefruit juice
1 ounce

TECHNIQUE
shake

GLASS
cocktail

Like many classics we still know today, the recipe for the Blood and Sand first appeared in the pages of *The Savoy Cocktail Book* by Harry Craddock, published in England in 1930. The color of blood-soaked dirt, thanks to the inclusion of Heering, a Danish cherry liqueur with a rich, earthy quality, the Blood and Sand is one of the rare classic cocktails that has Scotch as its base ingredient. The classic recipe calls for orange juice, and this is where I differ from the purists. I use grapefruit juice, which has just the right amount of sourness, sweetness, and bitterness to balance out almost any cocktail, and this drink is no exception.

Add everything to a cocktail shaker with ice.

Shake hard for 10 seconds or so, until the outside of the shaker starts to get frosty.

Fine strain into a chilled cocktail glass and garnish with a twist of **orange peel.**

PRO TIP: CHOOSING WHISKY
If you like smoky Scotch, this is a great drink to make as it works particularly well with that kind of flavor. For a pretty basic version, stick with something like Johnnie Walker Black Label, which is dryer and smokier than most blended Scotch whiskies, but if you want something really special, give it a try with Bowmore or Caol Ila single malt.

drinks just wanna have fun

The era before the great cocktail renaissance of the early 2000s is often called the "dark ages" of the cocktail. It was a time when fresh ingredients and proper technique were forsaken, and mixed drinks were seen only as the purview of bachelorette parties and cheesy nightclubs. A time before craft beer, before natural wine, before the whiskey boom, and before anyone outside of Oaxaca had ever heard of mezcal, let alone put it in a cocktail. Instead, Absolut vodka and Bacardi rum reigned supreme. Back then, bartenders were seen as performers more than masters of flavor and balance.

Many of the cocktails invented during this period have been left in the past where they belong, or maybe on the list at T.G.I. Friday's (a chain which, despite terrible cocktails, deserves a lot of credit for training countless professional bartenders in the 1980s and '90s). But during this time, the infant cocktail revival was just taking its first unsteady steps as visionary bartenders like Dale DeGroff (see Cosmopolitan, page 95) and Dick Bradsell (see Espresso Martini, page 96) were beginning to rediscover the lost art of mixology. Many of their brilliant concoctions have stood the test of time, inspiring subsequent generations of bartenders and repopularizing craft cocktails the world over.

Some drinks of the '70s, '80s, and '90s have also managed to maintain a kind of semi-ironic cultural cachet, evoking nostalgia for a time when people didn't take cocktails so damn seriously. To be honest, all the esoteric classics, bespoke craft spirits, and house-made bitters can get a bit tiresome. So, for this chapter, let's throw off the shackles of bartending orthodoxy for a moment and remember that, much like Cyndi Lauper, drinks just wanna have fun.

piña colada

dark rum

2 ounces

pineapple juice (see tip)

2 ounces

coco lópez cream of coconut

2 ounces

TECHNIQUE
blend

GLASS
highball

For me, the best Piña Colada is the simplest one, including only three ingredients: rum, pineapple juice, and cream of coconut, which is coconut milk that has been extracted, sweetened, and processed to form a thick syrup. Vegans and the lactose intolerant need not fret, because this version contains no dairy, relying instead on real coconut for that wonderful, creamy texture. If you can't find Coco López cream of coconut, you still have options! There are other brands on the market such as Coco Reàl, or you can make this drink with 2 ounces of coconut cream and 1 ounce of agave syrup instead of the Coco López.

Add everything to a blender with a big scoop of ice (enough to fill the glass you'll be drinking from).

Blend until the ice is totally pulverized.

Pour into the highball glass directly from the blender and garnish with a wedge of **pineapple** and a **maraschino cherry.**

PRO TIP: FRESH PINEAPPLE
This cocktail is at its best when you can get hold of fresh, ripe pineapple. Remove the skin and core and chop up the flesh into 2-inch chunks, saving the leaves for garnish. Replace the pineapple juice in this recipe with a cup of pineapple chunks added directly to the blender.

MAKE IT FOR COMPANY
Frozen drinks like this are great for parties because if you have a big enough blender, you can make a lot all at once, and the blender does all the work! Multiply the recipe by the number of drinks you want— just don't fill the blender more than halfway with liquid, and be sure you have at least as much ice as liquid by volume.

the origins of the piña colada

The term *piña colada* translates literally to *strained pineapple*—a traditional Caribbean preparation of fresh pineapple. Blended and strained, the juice is served over shaved ice for a brilliant tropical thirst quencher. Adding rum to this for a "Ron Piña" has been common across the Spanish-speaking Caribbean for ages. But in 1954, the brand-new Caribe Hilton Hotel in Puerto Rico, Hilton's first-ever international resort, introduced thousands of vacationing Americans to the joys of rum and pineapple.

A bartender at the Hilton by the name of Ramón "Monchito" Marrero Pérez had the idea of adding a can of Coco López, a newly invented brand of sweetened cream of coconut, to the Hilton's Ron Piña, and the Piña Colada as we know it today was born.

cosmopolitan

citrus vodka
1 ounce

cointreau or other orange liqueur/triple sec
1 ounce

lime juice
1 ounce

cranberry juice
1 ounce

TECHNIQUE
shake

GLASS
cocktail

The Cosmopolitan was created by Dale "King Cocktail" DeGroff, one of the primary progenitors of the cocktail revival, in the 1980s. But despite inventing the drink, it was not King Cocktail who made it famous. That achievement goes to one Carrie Bradshaw and the writers who created her for the HBO smash hit *Sex and the City,* which premiered in 1998. Thanks to Carrie's (and Miranda's, Charlotte's, and Samantha's) love of the Cosmo, it is now one of the world's most famous cocktails invented this side of Prohibition. While most modern recipes call for a little more vodka and a little less cranberry, I was originally taught this drink as an equal parts recipe, and it still holds up, especially with a good citrus-flavored vodka, which was all the rage in the '90s. For this drink I like to use Ketel One Citroen, but for a proper '90s vibe it's gotta be Absolut.

Add everything to a cocktail shaker filled with ice.

Shake hard for 10 seconds or so, until the outside of the shaker starts to get frosty.

Fine strain into a chilled cocktail glass and garnish with a twist of **orange peel.**

espresso martini

sweet **rich** **frothy**

irish whiskey

1 ounce

kahlúa or other coffee liqueur

1 ounce

freshly brewed espresso, chilled

1 ounce

TECHNIQUE
shake

GLASS
cocktail

Invented by legendary bartender Dick Bradsell in London in the 1980s, the Espresso Martini works because it incorporates a few of the most basic elements of any good cocktail: a base spirit (such as vodka), a sweet element (like coffee liqueur), and something either bitter or sour for balance (in this case fresh espresso). For this recipe, I've opted for Irish whiskey as a nod to the classic Irish Coffee. It's richer than vodka but still relatively light as far as whiskey goes, closer to the body of a quality vodka than a big, beefy Scotch, and less intensely flavored than bourbon, so it blends in well. Canadian whisky will also work, and for something a lot richer, try mezcal (my favorite) or a good dark rum, both of which pair beautifully with coffee.

Add everything to a cocktail shaker filled with ice.

Shake hard for 10 seconds or so, until the outside of the shaker starts to get frosty.

Fine strain into a chilled cocktail glass and garnish with 3 **espresso beans.**

PRO TIP: HOW TO TREAT YOUR COFFEE

Coffee is the key ingredient in this drink, so you can't make a good Espresso Martini without good coffee. Here are a couple of pointers to make sure your coffee cocktails turn out great every time:

• Do not try to use normal drip coffee or (gasp!) instant mix. They are too watery and simply won't work.

• If you don't have access to a proper espresso machine, a single shot from a Nespresso or other similar pod machine will do. Use the "short" setting so there's not too much liquid.

• Alternatively, you can buy a bunch of shots of espresso from your favorite café and save them in the fridge for a few hours until it's cocktail time. You could also try replacing the espresso with a cold brew concentrate, like Chameleon or Grady's.

japanese slipper

midori melon liqueur

1 ounce

cointreau or other orange liqueur/triple sec

1 ounce

lemon juice

1 ounce

TECHNIQUE
shake

GLASS
cocktail

This drink is a fluorescent-green, unabashedly fruity throwback to the 1980s. A simple combination of equal parts Midori, Cointreau, and lemon, the Japanese Slipper defies normal cocktail construction by using two different fruit liqueurs while omitting a base spirit such as vodka or whiskey. But while it's definitely on the sweeter side, the use of freshly squeezed lemon juice, not a common ingredient in the '80s, gives the Japanese Slipper all the freshness and balance it needs. As a bartender friend of mine said to me recently, "It's easy to make, super fun, bright green, and tasty as hell. What's not to love?"

Add everything to a cocktail shaker filled with ice.

Shake hard for 10 seconds or so, until the outside of the shaker starts to get frosty.

Fine strain into a chilled cocktail glass and garnish with a **maraschino cherry.**

VARIATION: JAPANESE SANDAL
To give this drink a little more balance and complexity, many bartenders add a shot of **gin** to the recipe. It will cut the sweetness of the cocktail, make it a little stronger, and give it some extra flavor while still retaining the essence of the original. **White rum** or **tequila** will work well, too, but you'll have to come up with your own names for those variations.

the origins of the japanese slipper

Midori, the Japanese melon liqueur, was first introduced in the United States in 1978. The occasion was the wrap party for *Saturday Night Fever* and the venue was New York's Studio 54, probably the world's most famous nightclub at the time. Lurid and lavish, Midori was made for the young, urban partygoers of the late '70s, when disco ruled the dance floor and this violently green liquid matched the eye shadow of the dancers.

A few years later, a young Frenchman named Jean-Paul Bourguignon was just hitting his stride as the bartender at Mietta's, Melbourne's number one restaurant at the time and a champion of Australia's nascent cocktail culture. Bourguignon, who had been trained at American-style cocktail bars in Paris, came up with the Japanese Slipper when a sales rep dropped off a bottle of Midori for him to play with. He combined it with Cointreau for a little French flair and fresh lemon for balance, garnishing it with a maraschino cherry.

After leaving the restaurant, Bourguignon spent the next twenty-odd years training bartenders and consulting for hospitality businesses all around Australia and the region, thus spreading the recipe for the Japanese Slipper and leading to its global recognition as a true modern classic.

french martini

  fruity · frothy · sweet

gin
1 ounce

**chambord
(see tip)**
1 ounce

dry vermouth
1 ounce

pineapple juice
1 ounce

TECHNIQUE
shake

GLASS
cocktail

The French Martini is a wonderful gateway cocktail for anyone wanting to experience the sophistication of the classics but in a sweet, fruity, and easy-to-drink format. Based on the French black raspberry liqueur Chambord, the French Martini comes out a lovely pink color, and the inclusion of pineapple juice gives it a delightfully fluffy texture when shaken. The most basic formula for a French Martini is simply equal parts vodka, Chambord, and pineapple juice, but to give it a little extra complexity and to honor the "martini" moniker, I've added dry vermouth to this recipe, and replaced the vodka with gin. The addition of gin also brings this recipe pretty close to the classic Clover Club cocktail (gin, lemon juice, raspberry syrup, and egg white). If you prefer to stick with the classic formula, just eliminate the vermouth and switch the gin for vodka.

Add everything to a cocktail shaker filled with ice.

Shake hard for 10 seconds or so, until the outside of the shaker starts to get frosty.

Fine strain into a chilled cocktail glass and garnish with **freeze-dried raspberries.**

PRO TIP: BERRY LIQUEURS
If you don't have Chambord on hand, any sweet berry-flavored liqueur like crème de mûre (blackberry) or crème de cassis (blackcurrant) will work. You could also use a homemade or store-bought raspberry syrup, as long as it's made with real fruit.

pornstar martini

**vanilla vodka
(see tip)**

¾ ounce

**passion fruit
liqueur (see tip)**

¾ ounce

lime juice

¾ ounce

simple syrup

¾ ounce

**pulp of
1 passion fruit**

*(or ¾ ounce of passion
fruit pulp from a can)*

sparkling rosé wine

to top

TECHNIQUE
shake

GLASS
cocktail

The Pornstar Martini was created in London in 2002 by Douglas Ankrah, owner of the London bars LAB and Townhouse. Ankrah is quoted as saying that the drink was originally called the Maverick Martini, inspired by a strip club called Mavericks Revue Bar in Cape Town, South Africa. This cocktail's combination of vanilla, passion fruit, and sparkling wine is stupidly tasty, and the presentation of this deliberately cheeky cocktail makes it a whole lot of fun. Mixed drinks have a long history of risqué names (Sex on the Beach, anyone?), and we are, of course, all adults here.

Add everything except the wine to a cocktail shaker filled with ice.

Shake hard for 10 seconds or so, until the outside of the shaker starts to get frosty.

Fine strain the contents of the shaker into a chilled cocktail glass. Top with sparkling rosé and garnish with half a **passion fruit.**

To serve, pour a shot glass of sparkling rosé to go alongside the drink as a sidecar.

PRO TIP: VANILLA VODKA
Vanilla-flavored vodka is one of those things you should have on hand if you like Espresso Martinis or White Russians, but it's not essential. If you don't want to buy a whole other bottle, there are some options for giving this drink the vanilla flavor it needs. Replace the simple syrup with a vanilla syrup or vanilla-flavored liqueur like Galliano Vanilla.

PRO TIP: PASSION FRUIT LIQUEUR
For the passion fruit liqueur, opt for a modern brand like Chinola. You can also replace the liqueur with a high-quality passion fruit–flavored syrup such as those produced by Monin or Liber & Co. If you go with this option, reduce the amount of simple syrup a little.

long island iced tea

vodka
¾ ounce

gin
¾ ounce

tequila
¾ ounce

white rum
¾ ounce

**cointreau or
other orange
liqueur/triple sec**
¾ ounce

lemon juice
¾ ounce

coca-cola
to top

TECHNIQUE
shake

GLASS
**pint glass or hurricane
glass (you need a large
glass for this one)**

Ah, the Long Island Iced Tea. What book of equal parts cocktails would be complete without the one recipe almost everyone knows? Just add one shot each of everything! A well-made Long Island Iced Tea has fresh lemon juice and the spice of Coke, which both offer some much-needed acidity and dilution to the boozy drink. So here's my recipe for the cocktail responsible for more missed college deadlines than any other, the mighty Long Island Iced Tea.

Add everything except the Coke to a cocktail shaker filled with ice.

Shake hard for 10 seconds or so, until the outside of the shaker starts to get frosty.

Fill a pint glass all the way to the top with ice, then add Coke until the glass is just shy of halfway full.

Slowly strain the contents of the shaker over the ice. Because the alcohol mixture has less density than the Coca-Cola, it should float on top of the Coke for a cool layered effect.

Garnish with a circle of **lime** and stir right before drinking to get the classic iced tea color.

white russian

vodka
1 ounce

kahlúa or other coffee liqueur
1 ounce

half-and-half
1 ounce

TECHNIQUE
build

GLASS
rocks

A combination of vodka, Kahlúa, and half-and-half, the White Russian is a dessert drink for the lazy. It's one of the very simplest recipes in this book. Sweet, creamy, and requiring absolutely no skill or knowledge of bartending technique, it's perfect for those times when you're feeling as unmotivated as a California stoner. The inclusion of vodka as a neutral base spirit essentially just makes the drink more alcoholic, so feel free to play around by replacing it with a spirit of your choice. Vanilla vodka works great, as will any kind of rum (including the spiced variety), pretty much any whiskey if it's not smoky, and even aged tequila, which pairs well with the coffee liqueur.

Grab whatever glass you have on hand, fill it with ice, add all the ingredients directly to the glass, and give it a quick stir.

If you want to be fancy, grate a little **nutmeg** over the top for garnish.

VARIATION: THE MUDSLIDE
One of the most popular dessert cocktails of the '80s and '90s was the Mudslide, essentially a boozy milkshake popularized by T.G.I. Friday's. Add to a blender **2 ounces heavy cream, 2 ounces vodka, 2 ounces Bailey's Irish Cream,** and **2 ounces Kahlúa.** Add **2 cups ice,** and blend until smooth. To make it look fancy, drizzle some **chocolate syrup** around the inside of the glass before pouring the drink.

frozen strawberry daiquiri

white rum

1 ounce

lime juice

1 ounce

strawberry liqueur

1 ounce

simple syrup

1 ounce

strawberries, either fresh with leaves removed, or frozen

½ cup

TECHNIQUE

blend

GLASS

margarita coupette or hurricane glass

The traditional daiquiri is a super-simple drink of white rum, fresh lime juice, and sugar. Incredibly refreshing and quite sour, it sits well within the realm of classy classic cocktails. But screw that—this is a party, so let's make it pink! Blenders are a great way to incorporate frozen or fresh fruit into your drinks without a lot of mess. This recipe will work just as well with any fruit you can get your hands on, so feel free to play around depending on what you can get—my favorite is mango! If you don't have any strawberry liqueur, you can use another berry liqueur, like Chambord (black raspberry) or crème de mûre (blackberry). You could also use strawberry jelly or a strawberry-flavored syrup, but if you do that, increase the amount of rum a little so your daiquiri isn't too weak.

Put everything in the blender and add 1 cup of ice.

Blend until smooth in texture, pour into a glass, and garnish with a fresh **strawberry** or fresh **mint.**

PRO TIP: BLEND IT LIKE YOU MEAN IT
To get the right consistency, it's important to use *lots* of ice, and don't overfill your blender with liquid. You'll need at least the same volume of ice as all the other ingredients, otherwise your drink will be watery and not that nice slushy texture. Never fill the blender more than halfway with liquid and fruit before you start adding ice.

MAKE IT FOR COMPANY
Frozen drinks are also perfect for making a lot of cocktails all at once—you just have to multiply the recipe ingredients by the number of drinks you want. A standard blender should be able to produce four or five cocktails at once, and even small personal blenders like the Nutri-bullet should get you at least two servings.

golden cadillac

cognac
1 ounce

white crème de cacao
1 ounce

galliano l'autentico (see tip)
1 ounce

heavy cream
1 ounce

TECHNIQUE
shake

GLASS
cocktail

The Golden Cadillac is most definitely a dessert drink, incorporating white chocolate liqueur and cream for a sweet and smooth after-dinner tipple. This cocktail incorporates Galliano L'Autentico, the old-school Italian herbal liqueur that was super popular in the 1970s. The story goes that the Golden Cadillac was created in 1952 at a bar called Poor Red's in El Dorado, California, when a honeymooning couple pulled up in shiny new gold Cadillac and asked the bartender to mix them up something unique. It's still on the menu to this day, if you happen to be cruising past. For this recipe, I've included brandy to give the drink a little extra depth, and because the Golden Cadillac is already pretty close to the classic Brandy Alexander, another cream drink that was popular in the 1970s, so I've sort of combined the two. But feel free to omit the brandy if you want to stick to the classic formula.

Add everything to a cocktail shaker filled with ice.

Shake hard for 10 seconds or so, until the outside of the shaker starts to get frosty.

Fine strain into a chilled cocktail glass and garnish by grating some **dark chocolate** over the top.

PRO TIP: GALLIANO
These days, Galliano Vanilla is much more common than the original Galliano L'Autentico, but it will not work as a replacement in this recipe! L'Autentico is much more herbal, giving this drink the depth and complexity it needs to really sing. If you can't find it, Yellow Chartreuse or another sweet, herbal liqueur like Strega or Bénédictine D.O.M. will work, too.

modern classics

110

modern bartenders love an equal parts cocktail. In fact some have become famous for them. Sam Ross, co-owner of bar Attaboy in New York, was named American Bartender of the Year in 2011. He's also a proud Melbourne boy like me, and we Aussies are pretty chuffed (to use an Australianism meaning *stoked*) to have one of our own so well regarded on the world stage. Sam and his team are known for creating "modern classics"—original cocktails that became known the world over, much like the old-school classics featured in chapter 3 (pages 68–87).

Some of Sam's most famous cocktails use the equal parts formula, including the Paper Plane (page 114) and the Praying Mantis (page 116). Many of the recipes in this chapter follow a similar pattern of a base spirit, plus something sweet, balanced with something bitter (like an amaro) and something dry like sherry or vermouth, and often sour citrus juice. By using this formula and playing around with the above elements, you can create an almost infinite number of modern classics.

During the early days of the cocktail renaissance, leading bartenders like Audrey Saunders and Joaquín Simó relied heavily on the equal parts formula to create riffs on classic cocktails, forming the base for modern mixology. Bars like Pegu Club and Milk & Honey revived classic cocktails and their associated culture with a renewed focus on high-quality, fresh ingredients and unfamiliar spirits. The recipes in this chapter tell that story and offer insight into the way professional bartenders come up with brilliant new drinks. All this goes to show that equal parts cocktail recipes are far from cheating; they are a critical way of making great drinks that's as relevant today as ever.

old cuban

dark rum

1 ounce

simple syrup

1 ounce

lime juice

1 ounce

angostura bitters

2 dashes

sparkling wine

1 ounce

fresh mint

8 leaves

TECHNIQUE
shake

GLASS
cocktail

This is a wonderful mash-up of a classic Champagne cocktail and a Mojito, combining some of the best elements of each drink for something that's rich, fun, delicious, and feels like a celebration. The Old Cuban comes from the mind of one of America's most influential bartenders, Audrey Saunders. Known as one of New York City's best, Saunders ran the legendary SoHo bar Pegu Club from 2005 to its closing in 2020. Pegu Club was hugely influential in popularizing forgotten classic cocktails, and much of modern mixology technique and style developed thanks to Saunders and her bar. The use of fresh mint in this drink gives it a wonderfully fresh scent, helped along by the inclusion of sparkling wine, those little bubbles lifting the minty aroma right out of the glass.

Add everything except the sparkling wine to a cocktail shaker filled with ice.

Shake hard for 10 seconds or so, until the outside of the shaker starts to get frosty.

Fine strain into a chilled cocktail glass, add the sparkling wine, and garnish with a **mint leaf.**

PRO TIP: GIVE IT A SMACK!
When using fresh mint for a garnish, you'll often see bartenders giving it a bit of a smack between their hands. This is done to release some of the aromatic oils and make it smell really nice on top of the drink. Simply lay the mint leaf flat on your open palm, and give it one good clap with the other hand before floating it on top of the cocktail.

paper plane

bourbon
1 ounce

aperol
1 ounce

amaro nonino
1 ounce

lemon juice
1 ounce

TECHNIQUE
shake

GLASS
cocktail

This equal parts cocktail, created by Melbourne-born Sam Ross, founder of Attaboy in New York, is one of the best-known modern classics in the world. The Paper Plane is bright and fresh thanks to plenty of lemon juice and comes out a beautiful orange color with a nice foamy head. It's the kind of drink that makes people say, "I'll have what she's having." So even if you're not much of a whiskey fan, give this drink a try. The oaky richness of bourbon really does wonders. But, like many drinks in this book, the recipe will also work well with other spirits such as brandy or dark rum.

Add everything to a cocktail shaker filled with ice.

Shake hard for 10 seconds or so, until the outside of the shaker starts to get frosty.

Fine strain into a chilled cocktail glass. See tip for garnish suggestions.

PRO TIP: <u>FUN WITH GARNISHES</u>
This is a drink that doesn't really need a garnish, but if you want to have some fun, make a tiny paper plane and clip it to the side with a baby clothes pin. Given the drink's bright orange color, green things will work well as garnishes, too, like a lemon leaf or a sprig of fresh mint.

praying mantis

islay single-malt scotch whisky (such as laphroaig)
1 ounce

gran classico bitter
1 ounce

lemon juice
1 ounce

sweetened ginger juice (recipe follows)
1 ounce

TECHNIQUE
shake

GLASS
cocktail

The Praying Mantis is my favorite of an entire series of equal parts cocktails created by Sam Ross and the Attaboy team at their bars in New York and Nashville. The foundation of these drinks is simple: a base spirit, plus an amaro of some kind, plus citrus juice, plus fresh ginger juice, all in equal amounts. These drinks work beautifully because the fresh ginger is so wonderfully spicy and aromatic, and the amaro lends depth and sweetness. The Praying Mantis comes from bartender and co-owner Brandon Bramhall of Attaboy in Nashville. I like the use of smoky Scotch, but it is still a refreshing, citrus-forward cocktail. As the team at Attaboy have done, you can riff on this formula endlessly, switching out the base spirit and the choice of amaro to your heart's content.

Add everything to a cocktail shaker filled with ice.

Shake hard for 10 seconds or so, until the outside of the shaker starts to get frosty.

Fine strain into a chilled cocktail glass, and garnish with a piece of **candied ginger** skewered on two toothpicks.

sweetened ginger juice

granulated sugar (or honey)
½ cup

boiling water
¼ cup

fresh ginger juice
½ cup

Juice enough fresh ginger to get ½ cup of juice (about 1 pound), or you can purchase it from your local juice shop or organic grocery store. In a 2-cup heatproof measuring cup or cocktail mixing glass, add the sugar (or replace with honey for an incredible ginger-honey version!). Pour in the boiling water and stir until a thick syrup forms. Add the ginger juice and continue to stir until the sugar is fully dissolved. Allow to cool fully before using. You can store this in a clean, airtight container in the fridge for up to 1 month.

what the hell is gran classico bitter?

I wanted to include the Praying Mantis for its use of Gran Classico Bitter, a delicious, soft, complex, and not overly bitter amaro produced by the folks at Tempus Fugit, who make some of the best cocktail ingredients in the world. It is based on a recipe for Italian Bitter of Turin from the 1860s. Originally produced under the name Torino Gran Classico, it's made with twenty-five aromatic herbs and roots, including wormwood, gentian, bitter orange, rhubarb, and hyssop. It's a pretty good substitute for any cocktail calling for Amer Picon (like the classic rye-based Brooklyn). On a hot day, add a shot of this to a big frosty glass of lager for a French Amer Bière. If you don't want to buy a whole new bottle of Gran Classico Bitter just for this recipe, you can replace it with another well-balanced amaro like Aperol, Nonino, or Montenegro.

jungle bird

tropical **bittersweet** **fruity**

blackstrap rum
1 ounce

campari
1 ounce

lime juice
1 ounce

pineapple juice
1 ounce

TECHNIQUE
shake

GLASS
rocks

While this cocktail was created in the 1970s, it sits firmly in the category of modern classics as a drink that's come back into fashion with the revival of midcentury tropical cocktails. The Jungle Bird is ideal for people who don't want their drinks too sweet. Think of it as a cross between a Mai Tai and a Negroni, the bitterness of Campari counterbalancing the sweet tropical flavors of rum and pineapple. I've modified the original recipe by eliminating the simple syrup and changing the proportions slightly, but I find it works perfectly as a bright, refreshing equal parts drink. Still, if this version is a little too bitter or sour for you, feel free to add a splash of simple syrup.

Add everything to a cocktail shaker filled with ice.

Shake hard for 10 seconds or so, until the outside of the shaker starts to get frosty.

Strain into a large rocks glass, top with ice, and garnish with **pineapple leaves** and a **maraschino cherry.**

PRO TIP: BLACKSTRAP RUM
While "blackstrap" is not a true designation of rum style, it's generally understood to be very dark in color and with a powerful molasses flavor profile. For this drink, that rich, dark, sweet rum character works particularly well, so brands like Goslings Black Seal and Cruzan Black Strap will offer the best results, but any dark, Jamaican-style rum is fine if that's what you have!

the origins of the jungle bird

Born in in 1948 in Penang, Malaysia, Ong Swee Teik, also known as Jeffrey Ong, became the beverage director at the Kuala Lumpur Hilton when it opened in 1973. Much like the resort in Puerto Rico where the Piña Colada (page 91) was invented, the Malaysian outpost of Hilton International wanted a welcome drink to offer its guests. Inspired by the hotel's Aviary Bar, which sported an enclosure of live tropical birds, Ong created the Jungle Bird as the Kuala Lumpur Hilton's signature cocktail. When Ong passed away in 2019, Penang's newspaper, *The Star*, hailed him as the creator of Malaysia's only internationally recognized classic cocktail.

The Jungle Bird has become a staple on tropical cocktail lists, as well as a great drink to recommend in any setting because the ingredients are easy to find and the recipe is simple. It's also perfect for people who want some tropical fun in their glass but prefer a drink less sweet than most classic rum cocktails.

jasmine

gin
1 ounce

campari
1 ounce

triple sec
1 ounce

lemon juice
1 ounce

TECHNIQUE
shake

GLASS
cocktail

The Jasmine is a wonderfully light, pretty, and balanced drink that's perfect for sunny afternoons and cocktail parties alike. Inspired by the classic White Lady cocktail of gin, triple sec, and lemon juice, here the addition of bittersweet Campari gives the drink a modern flavor profile and gorgeous pale pink color. If you like fresh pink grapefruit, you will love this cocktail with its refreshing, juicy, bittersweet, and aromatic qualities. Created by bartender Paul Harrington at the Townhouse Bar & Grill in Emeryville, California, and included in his 1998 book *Cocktail: The Drinks Bible for the 21st Century*, the Jasmine is one of the most recognized modern classics of the '90s. Harrington's original recipe calls for slightly more gin, and a touch less Campari and triple sec, but it works perfectly as an equal parts recipe.

Add everything to a cocktail shaker filled with ice.

Shake hard for 10 seconds or so, until the outside of the shaker starts to get frosty.

Fine strain into a chilled cocktail glass and garnish with a twist of **grapefruit peel** (lemon or orange peel will work, too!).

VARIATION: PERIODISTA DAIQUIRI
For a classic daiquiri-style version of the jasmine that's a bit on the sweeter side, switch the gin in the recipe above for **white rum,** the Campari for **apricot liqueur,** and the lemon juice for **lime juice.** This drink was said to be enjoyed by Earnest Hemingway during his years in Cuba.

la viña

boozy **complex** **dry**

rye whiskey
1 ounce

amaro nonino
1 ounce

cream sherry (see tip)
1 ounce

orange bitters
2 dashes

TECHNIQUE
stir

GLASS
cocktail

Okay, so maybe La Viña isn't exactly a modern classic known by bartenders the world over. But I think it should be, so here it is. There are many variations on the Manhattan out there, my favorite being the classic Brooklyn cocktail and the most famous modern version being the Red Hook. But neither of those are equal parts cocktails, while this wonderful drink from New York's Death & Co. works perfectly with even proportions. Created by co-owner Alex Day, this rich, whiskey-forward drink includes Amaro Nonino, a delicious Italian bittersweet liqueur with a rich nutty flavor, and cream sherry for balanced sweetness.

Add everything to a mixing glass, fill with ice, and stir until chilled.

Strain into a chilled cocktail glass and garnish with a **preserved cherry.**

PRO TIP: CREAM SHERRY
Cream sherry is the general name for sherry made by blending dryer styles, such as oloroso or fino, with sweeter styles such as Pedro Ximénez or Moscatel, offering something in between in terms of sweetness. The cream sherry category is named after the historically popular Bristol Cream label from sherry producer Bodegas Harveys. For the recipe on this page, Alex Day recommends using Lustau East India Solera Sherry, but any brand of quality cream sherry will work. A dry sherry like oloroso or fino will also work, just be aware that the cocktail will turn out less sweet.

naked and famous

mezcal
1 ounce

campari
1 ounce

yellow chartreuse
1 ounce

lime juice
1 ounce

orange bitters
2 dashes

TECHNIQUE
shake

GLASS
cocktail

Mezcal has made big waves in recent years as a base spirit for modern cocktails. The Naked and Famous, for example, takes the same four-ingredient equal parts formula we've seen again and again in this chapter, employing mezcal as the base. This drink comes from the prolific mind of Joaquín Simó, who was part of the opening bar team at New York's Death & Co., one of the most influential bars of the modern era. Simó describes the cocktail as a "bastard child born out of an illicit Oaxacan love affair between the classic Last Word and the Paper Plane." The result is a drink that's powerful in flavor and gorgeous in color, created specifically with equal parts in mind, no modifications required.

Add everything to a cocktail shaker filled with ice.

Shake hard for 10 seconds or so, until the outside of the shaker starts to get frosty.

Fine strain into a chilled cocktail glass and garnish with a twist of **grapefruit peel** (lemon or orange peel will work, too!).

what the hell is mezcal?

Like tequila, mezcal comes from Mexico (mostly from the state of Oaxaca) and is made from the fermented and distilled juice of the agave plant. But you can think of mezcal a little like tequila's grandparent. It's been around for longer, it's a bit rough around the edges and less refined than tequila, and it tends to have bigger, bolder flavors—often smoky, mineral, earthy, or intensely peppery. If you're the sort of drinker that prefers big flavors like IPA over lager, gin over vodka, and single malt over blended Scotch, like I do, then mezcal is for you. Mezcal also has a much broader range of flavors and styles than tequila, with a creamier, richer texture, and tends to be a bit higher in alcohol.

Mezcal has exploded in popularity recently, from a little-known regional spirit to something enjoyed all over the world. As with many things, you get what you pay for, and because mezcal is often made by hand, the good stuff is more expensive than standard spirits like bourbon or gin. So definitely don't go for the cheapest bottle on the shelf. A decent bottle of mezcal good enough for cocktails should run you about forty dollars. I recommend brands like Siete Misterios, Del Maguey, and Pierde Almas for cocktails. A good "joven" (unaged) mezcal made from the espadín agave and with the designation "artesanal" (artisanal) should be perfect. It's not too expensive or intense, but not crappy either. But mezcal is a huge category, so there's a whole world of flavors here to explore.

london calling

navy-strength gin
1 ounce

fino sherry
1 ounce

lemon juice
1 ounce

simple syrup
1 ounce

orange bitters
2 dashes

TECHNIQUE
shake

GLASS
cocktail

Just one sip of London Calling will be enough for you to understand the appeal of this complex and classically styled drink. It's also bright, refreshing, and easy to make. Created by Chris Jepson in 2002 at the London outpost of Milk & Honey, the London Calling has had a huge influence on modern bartending due to the inclusion of one key ingredient: sherry. This style of fortified wine from Spain appears only sporadically in classic cocktail recipes, as, like most wines, it is traditionally preferred as a stand-alone drink. But sherry has become a hugely important part of the modern cocktail revival. It offers complexity without adding too much extra alcohol or sweetness, and it also blends well with spirits, liqueurs, and other common cocktail ingredients, happy to sing as part of the choir. For this equal parts version of the London Calling, which has less gin than the original, I recommend using a high-alcohol "navy-strength" gin to really help its flavor punch through, but it's not critical, so normal gin will work fine, too.

Add everything to a cocktail shaker filled with ice.

Shake hard for 10 seconds or so, until the outside of the shaker starts to get frosty.

Fine strain into a chilled cocktail glass and garnish with a twist of **grapefruit peel** (lemon or orange will work, too!).

gin gin mule

gin
1 ounce

lime juice
1 ounce

ginger liqueur
1 ounce

ginger beer
to top

TECHNIQUE
build

GLASS
highball

Another of Audrey Saunders's most famous creations, the Gin Gin Mule is a great example of a modern take on what we call "tall" or "long" drinks—cocktails topped up with some kind of soda for a longer-lasting, more refreshing drinking experience. Here Saunders plays with the classic Moscow Mule recipe of vodka, lime, and ginger beer and gives it extra depth and aroma with the inclusion of fresh mint, gin, and ginger liqueur. For the ginger liqueur, I recommend King's Ginger or Sweetened Ginger Juice (page 116). Using fresh mint in drinks is a lot of fun because it smells and looks so good. In the summer months, it's easy to find at the store, but it's also really easy to grow, even if you only have a window box or some other kind of small space for gardening. As long as you can get plenty of direct sunlight, mint will go bananas in the warmer months, providing you with an endless supply of cocktail garnishes.

Add the gin, lime juice, and ginger liqueur to a chilled highball glass and fill with ice.

Top it up with ginger beer and give it a quick stir, then garnish with a big sprig of fresh **mint.**

white negroni

aromatic　bittersweet　complex

gin
1 ounce

off-dry vermouth
1 ounce

suze gentian liqueur
1 ounce

TECHNIQUE
build

GLASS
rocks

Credited to English bartender Wayne Collins, a leading figure in the London cocktail scene in the 1990s, the White Negroni is a perfect example of how modern bartenders have taken a tried-and-true classic cocktail and modified the ingredients to create something entirely new while maintaining an obvious connection to the original. In this case, the sweet vermouth of the classic Negroni is switched out for off-dry vermouth, which still provides sweetness but is lighter and more aromatic. The Campari is replaced with another bittersweet herbal liqueur called Suze. The combination of gin, off-dry vermouth, and Suze makes for a wonderfully light and floral style of Negroni. I find that this cocktail is at its best when made with savory gins that include salty ingredients like olive or seaweed, as that little hint of salt does wonders to enhance flavor. Try this recipe with something like Gray Whale Gin from California, Isle of Harris Gin from Scotland, or Newfoundland Distillery Seaweed Gin from Canada to see what I mean. Alternatively, you could add a barspoon of olive brine to your glass for a similar effect.

Add all of the ingredients to a chilled rocks glass, fill with ice (one nice big block if you have it), give it a quick stir, and garnish with a twist of fresh **lemon peel.**

VARIATION: WHITE MEZCAL NEGRONI
My favorite way to have this concoction is to replace the gin with **mezcal.** If you're a fan of mezcal, this is a wonderful way to enjoy it in cocktail form. Try it garnished with a twist of fresh pink grapefruit peel instead of lemon.

wonders of the world

Equal parts cocktail recipes don't just come from the bars of New York and London, or from the pages of old mixology books. They're used all over the world to showcase the unique ingredients of places from Guadalajara to Bangkok, and to express the creativity of modern bartenders from every walk of life.

One of the best things about being a bartender is that we're an international family. We tend to be pretty intrepid folks, often moving across the globe to ply our trade. It's one of those skills that can land you a job in pretty much any major city. I'm lucky enough to have friends in India, Europe, Southeast Asia, Mexico, and many other wonderful places, who represent the very best of international bartending.

So, for this chapter, I've reached out to my bartending brothers and sisters around the world, as well as the ones closer to home, to get their best equal parts cocktails. These drinks are a little more advanced than those in previous chapters, some requiring extra time and attention to detail or less common ingredients, but all fit into the equal parts formula.

You can think of this chapter as your final project—your master's thesis for equal parts cocktails. Here you'll find incredible flavors and wildly creative mixed drinks, created by bartenders I respect and admire, representing cultures and cuisines from across the globe.

jitterbug

bright **floral** **summery**

cachaça or white rum
1 ounce

elderflower liqueur
1 ounce

aperol
1 ounce

lime juice
1 ounce

TECHNIQUE
shake

GLASS
rocks

David Molyneux | The Everleigh | Melbourne, Australia

For more than a decade before it closed in 2025, the Everleigh was known as Australia's best bar for classic cocktails. This hugely influential venue provided a stage for bartenders like David Molyneux, who came up with this absolutely delicious equal parts cocktail during his time working there. The Jitterbug basically tastes like springtime in a glass. Complex, floral, light, and perfectly balanced, this is the kind of cocktail absolutely anyone will love at first sip. Here, the inclusion of high-quality elderflower liqueur is the key. Floral without being at all soapy or overly perfumed, it's a wonderful ingredient to have on your home bar. Dave's original recipe calls for gin, but I've replaced it with cachaça, the native rum of Brazil, for something a little different. But regular white rum, or pretty much any white spirit you have on hand, will work well, too.

Add everything to a cocktail shaker filled with ice.

Shake hard for 10 seconds or so, until the outside of the shaker starts to get frosty.

Strain into a rocks glass. Fill the glass with crushed ice and garnish with a sprig of fresh **mint.**

PRO TIP: CRUSHED ICE
The simplest way to crush ice is to wrap some cubes in a kitchen towel or a pillowcase and smash it with a wooden mallet or a rolling pin. You can also buy specialized ice-crushing bags and mallets from cocktail supply stores. If you're making drinks for a group, using a powerful blender or a specialized ice-crushing machine is an even better bet—otherwise you'll tire very quickly.

kalimotxo

sweet vermouth

1 ounce

red wine

1 ounce

aperol

1 ounce

lemon juice

1 ounce

coca-cola

to top

TECHNIQUE
build

GLASS
large wineglass

Dive Bars the World Over

The Kalimotxo is a simple combination of equal parts red wine and Coke, favored by backpackers, students, and other budget-conscious drinkers in many places around the world. It first became popular in the Basque region of Spain in the 1970s and has since spread to places like Chile, where it's called "Jote," and to South Africa, where it's known as "Katemba." It's a great way to make cheap red wine more refreshing and fun, even if it's past its prime. Here I've taken the basic recipe and made it more like a classic cocktail, which bartenders in places like Lisbon, Buenos Aires, and New York City have also done, adding Aperol for a bit of bright citrus and bitterness. If you want to try this with an Italian or Argentinian flavor, replace the Aperol with Fernet-Branca amaro—just be aware that the resulting cocktail will be a lot more bitter.

Add everything except the Coke directly to your wineglass.

Fill the glass with ice, top it up with Coke, and give it a stir.

Garnish with **lemon wheels.**

MAKE IT FOR COMPANY
Fill a pitcher with ice, then fill it to the halfway point with equal parts **sweet vermouth, red wine, Aperol,** and **lemon juice,** then top up with **Coke.** Serve by pouring it into wineglasses filled with ice and garnished with **lemon wheels.**

VARIATION: SANGRIA
To make something that resembles a more traditional sangria, replace the Coca-Cola in this recipe with dry **ginger ale** and garnish with slices of **orange.**

breakfast in tijuana

  fruity funky citrusy

mezcal

1 ounce

cointreau or other orange liqueur/triple sec

1 ounce

strawberry puree (see tip)

1 ounce

marmalade

1 ounce

lime juice

1 ounce

TECHNIQUE
shake

GLASS
rocks

Supawit Muttarattana | Dry Wave Cocktail Studio | Bangkok, Thailand

Bangkok has one of the most exciting and dynamic cocktail scenes in the world right now. One of the bartenders leading the charge is Supawit Muttarattana, cofounder of Dry Wave Cocktail Studio. Dry Wave's menu features what they call "Super Classics," which see two different classic cocktails combined to create something new—classic cocktail mash-ups, if you will. Supawit was kind enough to share with me the recipe for his Super Classic, Breakfast in Tijuana, a marriage of a Strawberry Mezcal Margarita and the well-known Breakfast Martini cocktail made with Cointreau and marmalade. The result is both fun and fruity while also complex and engaging, the combination of strawberries and marmalade creating something both rich and refreshing. I've modified the recipe slightly here to fit with the equal parts formula.

Add everything to a cocktail shaker filled with ice.

Shake hard for at least 10 seconds or so, until the outside of the shaker starts to get frosty. Because of the fruit in this drink, you'll need to give it a really good shake to make sure everything is properly combined!

Strain over ice into a rocks glass rimmed with **kosher salt** (see the Pro Tip on page 65). Garnish with a fresh **strawberry.**

PRO TIP: STRAWBERRY PUREE
To make a strawberry puree, get some fresh strawberries (or thawed frozen ones) and process in a blender until smooth. You can also use a store-bought cocktail puree like Monin or Finest Call.

If you can't be bothered with all that, you can simply add a few fresh strawberries to your cocktail shaker before you add the other ingredients and mash them up with a muddling stick or the back of a spoon.

buckskin playmate

  **complex**

**barrel-proof
rye whiskey**

¾ ounce

**barrel-proof
bourbon**

¾ ounce

sweet vermouth

¾ ounce

**rainwater madeira
(see below)**

¾ ounce

orange bitters

2 dashes

angostura bitters

2 dashes

absinthe

2 dashes

TECHNIQUE
stir

GLASS
rocks

Opening Team | Ticonderoga Club | Atlanta, Georgia

Greg Best, owner of Atlanta's Ticonderoga Club, is a mentor of mine. He and his team make the kind of drinks I love: simple, well-balanced, delicious, and served with a big ol' side of Southern hospitality. Greg describes this boozy cocktail inspired by the literary works and drinking traditions of early America as "a very likeable addition to the brooding, whiskey-driven cocktail arsenal." The "barrel-proof" whiskeys in this recipe are bottled at full strength right out of the barrel, not diluted with water, which makes for a powerful, high-alcohol cocktail. But feel free to use whatever whiskeys you have on hand, or even other dark spirits like añejo tequila, dark rum, or brandy.

Add everything to a mixing glass filled with ice.

Stir until chilled, then strain into a chilled rocks glass. Garnish with a big twist of **lemon peel.**

what the hell is rainwater madeira?

Rainwater Madeira is a lighter, drier style of the classic fortified wine produced on the Portuguese island of Madeira and, like dry sherry, is a wonderful cocktail ingredient. In this recipe, it helps to counterbalance the sweeter and heavier elements. The brand Henriques & Henriques is the easiest one to find. Fino sherry will work in a pinch, too.

buckley's chance

amaro montenegro
1 ounce

heering cherry liqueur
1 ounce

lemon juice
1 ounce

angostura bitters
1 dash

orange bitters
2 dashes

TECHNIQUE
shake

GLASS
cocktail

Hayden Lambert | Above Board | Melbourne, Australia

Hayden Lambert is one of the world's most knowledgeable bartenders. His bar Above Board in Melbourne takes inspiration from Japan's minimalist cocktail counters: There's no back bar, no wine list, no snack menu, and very few seats. Here, it's all about the cocktails. Hayden's approach is classic—no outlandish, molecular techniques or esoteric ingredients, just great combinations of good booze, perfectly balanced and presented with a smile. This bright, refreshing, and complex drink is incredibly simple to make, and it's a perfect way to use some of the less common ingredients that appear in other recipes in this book. It's also not as strong in alcohol as most cocktails, and with many people reducing their booze consumption these days, it's always good to have a couple of low-alcohol recipes up your sleeve.

Add everything to a cocktail shaker filled with ice.

Shake hard for 10 seconds or so, until the outside of the shaker starts to get frosty.

Fine strain into a chilled cocktail glass—no garnish required.

foo fighters

bittersweet · herbal · rich

añejo tequila

1 ounce

fernet-branca

1 ounce

frangelico

1 ounce

TECHNIQUE
stir

GLASS
rocks

Peter Chua | Night Hawk | Singapore

Ordering a shot of Fernet-Branca at a bar is sometimes called the "bartender's handshake"—or an unofficial way of letting the folks serving you know that you work in the bar industry. Fernet is an intensely bitter and vegetal style of amaro and definitely not to everyone's taste. Personally, straight Fernet is too bitter for me, but I do love it mixed in cocktails. At Peter Chua's bar Night Hawk in Singapore, many of his guests agree with me. So, to ease people into drinking Fernet, Peter created his Foo Fighters cocktail. You can think of the Foo Fighters as a bittersweet and herbal twist on the Godfather (page 49). In many ways, it's also a variation of the classic Old Fashioned, with the Frangelico hazelnut liqueur acting as the sweetener, and the Fernet replacing the bitters for depth, complexity, and balance. Peter's original version calls for rye whiskey, but I've replaced it here with añejo tequila for something a little different. This recipe will also work with any well-aged spirit you prefer, such as dark rum or bourbon.

Add everything to a mixing glass filled with ice.

Stir until chilled, then strain into a chilled rocks glass over a nice chunk of ice and garnish with a twist of **lemon peel.**

ola verde

london dry gin

¾ ounce

pisco acholado

¾ ounce

suze gentian liqueur

¾ ounce

snap pea syrup (recipe follows)

¾ ounce

lime juice

¾ ounce

TECHNIQUE
shake

GLASS
cocktail

Ivy Mix | Leyenda | Brooklyn, New York

Ivy Mix is considered to be one of America's foremost experts on the spirits of Latin America, as well as one of the world's best bartenders. Her bar Leyenda in Brooklyn, New York, which closed after ten years in 2025, is credited with helping start the current tequila and mezcal craze sweeping the country (and the world), and her book *Spirits of Latin America* is one of the very best English-language guides to the incredible native spirits of that region. Ivy originally created this drink for Leyenda, but it never ended up on the menu. It's a great example of using fresh, savory, green ingredients to add an interesting and modern element to a mixed drink. The inclusion of gin, gentian liqueur, pisco, and sugar snap peas makes drinking this cocktail feel like standing in a garden in the middle of summer.

Add everything to a cocktail shaker filled with ice.

Shake hard for 10 seconds or so, until the outside of the shaker starts to get frosty.

Strain into a chilled cocktail glass and garnish with a fresh **sugar snap pea.**

what the hell is suze?

Suze is the most famous brand of bittersweet amaro from a class called gentian liqueurs. Gentian is a bitter plant that grows in alpine regions of Europe and has been used for medicinal purposes for thousands of years. Gentian liqueurs tend to have an intense, floral bitterness that is offset with sugar and other flavorings. These liqueurs, little known outside of Europe until relatively recently, have become a favorite tool in the modern bartending arsenal, adding a huge amount of depth and complexity to cocktails as well as counterbalancing sweeter ingredients with that lovely floral bitterness.

snap pea syrup

granulated sugar
¾ cup

water
¾ cup

**roughly chopped
sugar snap peas**
1 cup

In a small saucepan over medium heat, stir the granulated sugar and water together until the sugar is fully dissolved. Allow the mixture to cool to room temperature before transferring it to a blender.

Meanwhile, bring another small pot of water to boil over high heat, and fill a medium bowl with ice and water to make an ice bath. Add the snap peas to the boiling water and cook for 1 minute. Strain the peas and quickly add them to the ice bath. Allow the peas to cool fully.

Strain the peas and add them to the blender with the cooled syrup. Blend the syrup and peas together, then strain out any solids with a fine strainer.

The syrup can be stored in a clean, airtight glass container in the refrigerator for up to a month.

semper fizz

**contemporary gin
(see page 29)**

⅔ ounce

off-dry vermouth

⅔ ounce

**falernum
(see below)**

⅔ ounce

**pink grapefruit
juice**

⅔ ounce

lime juice

⅔ ounce

egg white
*(see page 41 for
alternatives)*

⅔ ounce

orange bitters

2 dashes

tonic water

to top

TECHNIQUE
shake

GLASS
highball

Arijit Bose | New Delhi, India

This drink is a fun, tropical, and refreshing twist on the classic gin fizz, adapted from a recipe by my friend Arijit Bose. Known in global bartending circles as "The Prince of India," Arijit has had a long and storied career as one of South Asia's most influential bar personalities. This recipe comes from his time as brand ambassador for German gin brand Monkey 47—a wonderful example of contemporary gin. A fizz is a cocktail shaken with egg white and then topped with soda for a frothy, bubbly, silky texture. It's really fun to make and even more fun to drink. But if you don't want to mess with egg whites, just leave them out and serve this drink over ice instead. If gin isn't to your liking, try it with another white spirit, like vodka, white rum, or tequila.

Add everything except the tonic water to a cocktail shaker filled with ice.

Shake hard for 10 seconds or so, until the outside of the shaker starts to get frosty.

Fine strain into a highball glass with no ice.

Carefully top with tonic water. If you do this just right, you should be able to get the froth to come right up over the edge of the glass without spilling over!

Garnish with a twist of **grapefruit peel.**

what the hell is falernum?

Falernum is a spiced syrup hailing from the Caribbean that includes all sorts of delicious, aromatic ingredients like almond, lime peel, Jamaican allspice, and ginger. There are plenty of good commercial brands you can buy ready-made—I recommend Fee Brothers—but there are also some great recipes online for homemade falernum that will really take your tropical cocktails to the next level.

divino daiquiri

planteray stiggins' fancy pineapple rum

1 ounce

tempus fugit crème de banane (see tip)

1 ounce

pineapple juice

1 ounce

lime juice

1 ounce

TECHNIQUE
shake

GLASS
cocktail

Alejandra de Aguinaga | El Gallo Altanero | Guadalajara, Mexico

El Gallo Altanero, a tiny speakeasy in Guadalajara, is a temple to all things agave, with hundreds of bottles of tequila and mezcal on offer. And Alejandra de Aguinaga, born and raised in Guadalajara, is an important part of the team making this little bar one of the world's best places to drink. The recipe Alejandra kindly shared with me is a well-balanced riff on the classic daiquiri, taken to the next level with the tropical flavors of banana and pineapple, and a generous foamy texture. "It has the spirit of a hot afternoon with a floral shirt and sandals, the ocean breeze in your hair and not a care in the world," she says. "It's refreshing and joyful, with the clear intention to celebrate simplicity done right." I've modified Alejandra's recipe to include ingredients that are easier to locate, but you can see her original version below.

Add everything to a cocktail shaker filled with ice.

Shake hard for 10 seconds or so, until the outside of the shaker starts to get frosty.

Fine strain into a chilled cocktail glass and garnish with a wedge of **lime.**

PRO TIP: BANANA LIQUEUR
Most banana liqueurs are a sugary, artificial mess, but Tempus Fugit makes a good one that's natural tasting and not too sweet. It will make a big difference! If you can find some kind of artisanal banana-infused rum or eau-de-vie that's not too sweet, that will work, too!

VARIATION: ALEJANDRA'S VERSION
Alejandra's original recipe called for a couple of craft spirits that are hard to find outside of Mexico. But if you want to make it exactly her way, the recipe is ¾ ounce each of **Satvrnal Banana, Atávica Tepache Spirit, simple syrup,** and **lime juice.** Satvrnal Banana is a banana-infused white rum from the craft distillery Satvrnal in the state of Jalisco, and Atávica Tepache Spirit is a fermented beverage made from the peel of pineapples, also produced in Jalisco.

tsukikage martini

  classy dry aromatic

the hachi imo shōchū
1 ounce

fino sherry
1 ounce

off-dry vermouth
1 ounce

orange bitters
2 dashes

TECHNIQUE
stir

GLASS
cocktail

Stefano Bussi | The Aubrey at the Mandarin Oriental Hotel | Hong Kong, China

The Aubrey bar at the Mandarin Oriental Hotel Hong Kong is stunningly appointed in green velvet and gold, like something from a Gatsby-meets-Alice-in-Wonderland fever dream. The cocktails here are classically styled with a Japanese twist, employing a raft of traditional Japanese products not often seen outside the Land of the Rising Sun. These include things like awamori (distilled from indica rice in Okinawa), shōchū (the traditional Japanese spirit distilled from rice, barley, sweet potato, or brown sugar), umeshu (a liqueur made by steeping underripe ume plums in shōchū), and the spectacular whiskies the Japanese have borrowed from Scotland and made their own. This martini is a recent addition to the Aubrey's menu and is a modern spin on the classic Bamboo cocktail.

Add everything to a mixing glass filled with ice.

Stir until chilled, then strain into a chilled cocktail glass and garnish with a twist of **lemon peel** and a **sakura** (Japanese cherry blossom) or other edible flower.

VARIATION: THE CLASSIC BAMBOO
Said to have been invented in Japan in the late 1800s by German American bartender Louis Eppinger at the Grand Hotel in Yokohama, the Bamboo is perhaps the most famous sherry-based cocktail. Much like a lot of simple classics, the Bamboo has many variations, but this version comes from the 1908 edition of William Boothby's *The World's Drinks and How to Mix Them.*

This formula will be dry and bracing, perfect for a predinner apéritif. If you want it a little sweeter, add 1 ounce of sweet vermouth.

Dry vermouth, 1 ounce

Fino sherry, 1 ounce

Orange bitters, 2 dashes

Angostura bitters, 1 dash

TECHNIQUE: Stir
GLASS: Cocktail
Add everything to a mixing glass filled with ice.

Stir until chilled, then strain into a chilled cocktail glass and garnish with a twist of **lemon peel.**

further reading

Here are some recommendations to explore the ingredients and ideas found in this book a little deeper and to take your next steps into the world of cocktail creation.

classic cocktails

If you want to explore more of the kind of classic cocktails covered in the first couple of chapters of this book, *The Cocktail Bible: An A–Z of Two Hundred Classic and Contemporary Cocktails with Anecdotes for the Curious and Techniques for the Adventurous* is a great reference to have on hand, covering many of history's most famous cocktails in an easy to understand, no-frills format.

japanese liquors and cocktails

The Way of the Cocktail: Japanese Traditions, Techniques, and Recipes, by Julia Momosé is an incredible book that will guide you through Japanese customs of eating and drinking, the country's cocktail history, bartending techniques particular to the region, and the native beverages of Japan before diving into seasonal recipes defined by the Japanese philosophy of wa, which emphasizes harmony and unity.

modern cocktails

Death & Co.: Modern Classic Cocktails, with More than 500 Recipes, by Alex Day, David Kaplan, and Nick Fauchald, is a wonderful insight into modern cocktail creation, and how we get from classics like the Manhattan and the Whiskey Sour to the modern versions in the chapters of this book.

rum and tropical cocktails

Smuggler's Cove in San Francisco is considered by many to be the best tropicana cocktail bar in the world. *Smuggler's Cove: Exotic Cocktails, Rum, and the Cult of Tiki,* by Martin Cate with Rebecca Cate, is a fantastic guide to both the history of rum and tropicana in America and how to make world-class tropical cocktails.

Another favorite of mine is Jeff Berry's *Beachbum Berry's Potions of the Caribbean,* where I've found so many great stories and recipes, including the origin of the Piña Colada and the Mai Tai, as referenced in this book.

sherry

If you want to learn more about this wonderful and historically influential class of wine, grab a copy of Talia Baiocchi's excellent book *Sherry: A Modern Guide to the Wine World's Best-Kept Secret, with Cocktails and Recipes.* It's my go-to reference for this fascinating and delicious drink.

tequila, mezcal, pisco, and cachaça

Ivy Mix's *Spirits of Latin America: A Celebration of Culture & Cocktails, with 100 Recipes from Leyenda & Beyond* is probably the best English-language guide to these wonderful spirits, the people and places from which they come, and how to incorporate them into easy but really creative cocktails.

Agave Spirits: The Past, Present, and Future of Mezcals, by Gary Nabhan and David Suro Piñera, is another great read for a deep dive on mezcal.

advanced home bartending

And, of course, I have to recommend my wife Cara Devine's fantastic new book on taking your at-home bartending skills to the next level. *Behind the Home Bar: The Essential Guide to Making Cocktails at Home* is an easy-to-follow guide on advanced cocktail-making techniques like infusions, homemade syrups, fermentations, and all sorts of other fun methods if you want to get really serious about making drinks at home the way they do in the world's top cocktail bars. Her YouTube Channel, *Behind the Bar with Cara Devine,* is also a great place to go for heaps of delicious cocktail recipes and explanations of various spirits (you might see me on there every once in a while, too!).

acknowledgments

First, I would like to acknowledge that I live, drink, and write on the unceded lands of the Wurundjeri people of the Kulin Nation who have cared for this place since time immemorial, and I pay my deepest respects to their elders past and present.

To my mama, Susanna, and my papa, Ian, thank you for raising me with a red pen in hand and for reading to me every night, and to my stepfather, Peter, thanks for always encouraging me to follow a career in writing.

To my agent, Katherine Cowles, thank you for being in my corner, and to my editor, Claire Yee at Ten Speed, thank you for being an absolute pleasure to work with and guiding me through the process. To Lizzie Allen and the rest of the design team at Ten Speed, thank you for making this book look so beautiful, and to Kris Paulsen, thank you for your brilliant photos for this project.

To Greg Best, Ivy Mix, Arijit Bose, Alejandra de Aguinaga, Hayden Lambert, Peter Chua, Supawit Muttarattana, David Molyneux, and Stefano Bussi, thank you so much for your contributions to this book.

To my editors at *PUNCH*, thank you for putting me forward to write for Ten Speed—I can't think of a better endorsement.

To my Melbourne bartending family, thank you for helping me test and develop these recipes, with special thanks to John Hallett at Goodwater; Elijah at the Everleigh; Oisin, Axel, and the rest of the team at the Black Pearl; my Catfish kittens; and the whole Goodwater team for allowing me to prioritize this project.

To Nathan Beasley, all my thanks for being the walking encyclopedia of cocktail knowledge and all-around awesome human that you are. And to Lucien, thank you for your friendship and constant encouragement. To all my siblings, thank you for being tireless cheerleaders, and to Besha in particular, thank you for being the best drinking buddy and the best mentor a guy could ask for.

To my wife, Cara, thank you for everything you do, everything you are, and all of your encouragement and advice. And to Thelma, thanks for being my constant floofy companion.

about the author

Fred Siggins is a writer and spirits expert based in Melbourne, Australia. His writing on drinks and bar culture can be found in various local and international publications including *T: The New York Times Style Magazine Australia, Halliday Wine Companion, PUNCH, Good Food,* and *Boothby.* A twenty-five-year veteran of the hospitality and drinks industry, Fred has worked as a chef, manager, brand executive, and bartender, including many years at Melbourne cocktail institution Black Pearl. He is also a co-owner of Melbourne cocktail and whiskey bar Goodwater.

index

TEN SPEED PRESS
An imprint of the Crown Publishing Group
A division of Penguin Random House LLC
1745 Broadway
New York, NY 10019
tenspeed.com
penguinrandomhouse.com

Typefaces: Optimo's Plain and Family Type's Fazer

Library of Congress Cataloging-in-Publication Data
Names: Siggins, Fred, 1981– author.
Title: Equal parts cocktails : the simple ratio for spectacular drinks / by Fred Siggins.
Identifiers: LCCN 2025033835 (print) | LCCN 2025033836 (ebook) ISBN 9780593838815 (hardcover) | ISBN 9780593838822 (ebook)
Subjects: LCSH: Cocktails
Classification: LCC TX951 .S567 2026 (print) | LCC TX951 (ebook)
LC record available at https://lccn.loc.gov/2025033835
LC ebook record available at https://lccn.loc.gov/2025033836

Hardcover ISBN 978-0-593-83881-5
Ebook ISBN 978-0-593-83882-2

Editor: Claire Yee | Production editor: Taylor Teague
Designer: Lizzie Allen | Production designers: Mari Gill and Faith Hague
Production: Jane Chinn | Prepress color manager: Hannah Hunt
Copy editor: Mark McCauslin | Proofreader: Sigi Nacson
Indexer: Ken DellaPenta
Publicist: Lauren Chung | Marketer: Andrea Portanova

Manufactured in China

10 9 8 7 6 5 4 3 2 1

First Edition

The authorized representative in the EU for product safety and compliance is Penguin Random House Ireland, Morrison Chambers, 32 Nassau Street, Dublin D02 YH68, Ireland, https://eu-contact.penguin.ie.